SLEEP
AND
OTHER
THINGS
SHAPED
LIKE
DEATH
JOSHUA TOOL

PROLOGUE

there is a consequence to human consciousness.
a duality, that on one end, begs a great darkness. as to soak
in the straits of self and knowing, is enough to drive any
aware soul towards the cliffs of insanity. as where its counter
is only to be matched, by the sharp split and hard search for
some sort of blissful beacon. an alleviation of euphoria, a
semblance of hope— such as love, drugs, sex etc.,
and then, there is an in-between...

a liminal boredom. call it a large stone in your pocket.
weighing you down slowly, until you are utterly paralyzed by
the weight. the steady numb that is without contrasting relief.
these are the only options. seemingly.

poet and author joshua tool finds the plagues of promise and
problem and purges such paradox into word paintings with
playful pen on painful pages. somehow finding comfort and
great humbling from the idea of death and mortality,
but also completely destroyed by it.
leading to depression, alcohol abuse and self annihilation.

as any artistic endeavor, this is an attempt at catharsis.
a reach at connection. a vow of wishful conviction,
and a scream for change!

moreover, within the structure and deconstruction of his
poetry; this book, like any honest art,
you will feel it in your bones. in your teeth. in your sleep.
this three year collection by *tool*, is an alchemistic amalgam
of all things that burn the body

TABLE OF CONTENTS

s l e e p & other things shaped like death

| ribcage |

things do not live here
in the space between us
the quiet miles of stale air
the sky; an open blue wound

its distance echoes of omissive heartbeats
a murmur of orphaned organs
and my state i.d. card is marked—
with a little pink heart
for donor

as if; after this
i will have something left to give

| you |

still unnumbered
the stars like mosquitoes
or the breaths i've held between wishes
it doesn't count if you say it out loud
33 candles and counting
yet still unnumbered
how many times
i've thought about...

you

| the return of the snowbird |

cryonic flocks
of suspended bathing birds
in iceblink and canceled star
over flash frozen ivory as levitating lure
for canceled shadow
to peak
in iced wings and glazed feather
their nimbus grin preserved in frost
to cancel sun
in carrion circles
of carcass and concrete clouds
and fly again
in the carnage of *february*

| cognitive dissonance |

my compartments;
my compartments are color coded
with lead paint
some are shaped like morgue drawers
and others shaped like a drink worn neat

some are transparent
the rest are caked with layered aberrance
cold to the touch
a varnished carcass
a lush

chipped like my teeth as they open crooked
on flimsy trim and worn tracks
like i forgot to account
for how they would weigh when they became wet

damped down and dripping
flooded to the brim
i reorganize them every day
to make room for the new things that i want to keep in

until i don't
and i implode
and i don't know if i will ever be full
but i keep filling and spilling until my brain has no hold
and where to put this, i don't really know

my compartments are color coded
and the one for you
is painted

gold.

| dry erase |

it is back to the basics
the kind of pencil poems that are finished with erasers
my broken throat and your dumb smirking stare

this is the part where you squeeze in-between my legs
so we can both watch t.v. while i brush your hair

this is the part, where we lay stiff and still
to watch the garden grow from the window sill
as we find the parts of our bodies that itch
and knead our nubby nails, dermal deep to carve a niche

this is the part where i read your lips
illuminated lowly in the lamp light

this is a poem about us
laying awake
all night

| ctrl + alt + delete |

'til nascency is clad anew
we wear numbers
where names should be
neutered seeds
counterclockwise eunuchs
with hearts of stone to sharpen teeth

'til genesis regenerate
we gentrify everything
our sweet will be
sweat to death
necropolis of honeybee

'til nascency is clad anew
we shall be
a stitch in times' embroidery
just strings of light
unraveling

| scared sober|

i got too drunk again last night
nuanced and dizzy and spinning
stupidly puking in the dark

but maybe art, is meant to be regurgitated
or maybe exploring addiction, is to be appreciated
or maybe it's just a reason,

to write
a love note—
from the ones that meant it the most
but nobody heard the terror

| long division |

akimbo
as you stalled
my stare down the frame of the narrowing hall

folded lips like a paper swan
our distance grew short
like my temper
avoiding fights lengthened twice as long

so i saunter, wander, mosey on
grab your hips, lips, and kiss your yawn

are we mad or bored, or both?

maybe safely crazy's better off
than not to have our love at all

well;
maybe

| hushed as cotton |

flap and fold,
the fresh of linen wind
spring forward;
the lily and the light

under bower and beauty
of book and brook
in reverie
of cool river trickled toes
as dewy eyes break mist
in late shallow shadows

to sit and sip,
the nectarines sweet
of drupe's dense drip
from trees green grip
and orange and pink all around me

to remember—
as any a formidable frost
atweel thaw kind and keen

| as understood you will become |

i am
become delicate
skin scabbed to peel in pink
a blushing molt
i am
brandished in rosy cheek
and stuttered speech
in a room of drinks
i am
become bruising peach
i am become death
the before and hereafter
to rise
cauterized
to hold you clean
in fiery reach
caramelize the bittersweet

i am become delicate
because you are

| breakfast at the reef |

fidget the forked tongue of young love
serpent swaddled
thrown out with the bath water
to leave my boiled husk, soft and warm
and sweet
and weak

doing everything i can
to keep these snakes appeased
so i lather, rinse, repeat
yet there is still soap in my eyes
and i can barely breathe

| refraction test |

i see you in everything
to the moon and back
and i am
punished in it's pareidolia

this heartache
is a quiet knife : with two sides
as i see you
in everything
to the moon and back
and it is always something leaving

| inuit kisses |

rosy ration
speckled freckle
twitchy bridge
of button nose

touché tickle
playful sparring
this is how
we love & spoke

bumping beaks
silent speech
grazing sniffers
bopping bones

nostril nudging
gilded gaze;

with caring kiss
of *eskimo*

| five o'clock |

as it were,
blenched the golden beet
in full wince of colour
a silk stripped sun, in acid and stone
bleached as bone
or spotted glass

wherein you lather
in over-correcting shadow
marking space with unseen verbs

like;
hide.
run.
or sleep...

[or age;

] or tremble

| double-barreled |

raised by domesticated wolves
innately, i am
a trembling beg
with birthdays,
now becoming oak-aged

a duality : designed as a drink
drafts a war inside of me

domesticated wolves
habitual : with dulled teeth
salivating for salvation

trading love bites for new highs
be it blood, money, or beer
i become what i most fear
a trembling beg
and then all bets are off

| from the frozen section |

i am packaged,
with a perforated heart
a discounted dish—
picked from the frozen section

consumer friendly
and ripe to rip open
that sawing cardboard sound—

to nuke and consume
to heat like a hearth
and let rest—

before eating
as to not scorch your tongue

love notes; are now—
just microwave directions
on the back of the box

and this seemed to be much easier
when i was only cooking for one

| sweet helen |

sprung shut
a clasp brought bare of twined fingers
our knuckles were;
utensils
to ingest
the space remaining
and lock the forgotten within our palms

twenty pointy reasons to not let go
twenty more reasons to feel your soul
an experiment of lips
one million nerves now puzzled to fit

gentle energy
in delicate waiting
as words escape me
and air and knowing and noun

this is not a place to name
nor to speak aloud
something this prudently poetic
inherently human
divinely fortuitous
simply goes : without saying

| sex and stranger sugars |

my friends are always partying
as i become more stranger to myself—
in masturbation swan song

with heavy beak and hollow bones
i never got the hang of keeping things alive
like trying to garden in church clothes
just turning dirt
with holy ghosts

mirroring a magniloquent mannequin
with all of these borrowed teeth
so you can never tell me,
that i'm not smiling

not even stopping to help the nuns cross the street
brumal born, i play for keeps
and oh, what great harvest it was
for rainbow chard and mustard greens

my friends are always partying
as i fall apart
in a cup of tea

| paste and pity |

bathetic as the common cold
ubiquitous as growing old
like glittered glue on open wounds
your scars screamed pink but sparkled blue

this is my pursuit in purge
acidic words in every verse
burning heart in fluxing flame
to build a home inside my name

this
is craft time
the copy-paste of scattered mind
i run with scissors and two left shoes
a half built bridge just out of view

how many *popsicle-sticks* will i need to use
to finally
get over you?

| cloud cough |

the silent flood
in frozen white tide
as clandestine crystalline
subtle fall on morning porch
to bright the world in blank flake
whisper wind on deaf ground
and canceled plan
mother earth takes a sick day

the silent flood
in frozen white tide
as clandestine crystalline
subtle fall on morning porch
to bright the world in blank flake

| hiraeth |

within the liminal of inkhorn luster
and temperamental pen
i write down my reliable
inside of broken hymns

like leaving the home i'd built
but had only meant to rent
so i sweep and clean and bleach
'til no fingerprint is left

i look over to my right
and then back onto the west
without a steady address
returned letters i'd been sent

i'll be seeing you around
inside that changing permanence
with every pocket turned
but with even more to spend

| clutter |

how pedestrian of me
to break down days into microwave meals
to cut my work hands on lottery tickets
sleeping on a pile of unfolded laundry

too sore to run my hobbies down
as passion falls impertinent
plagued by the phalanx of *bingo halls*
i am just trying to expand my free space
but my dabber's run dry
a commentary on what i have prioritized

will it be my hands again tomorrow
that are stained with red corrections?
will they be too blistered, to erase any mistakes?
too shaky, to remember everyone's birthday
they very well might be.
and the microwave rang
but i washed my hands before i ate

| arm rest |

perhaps it was my length in stretch
in morning time of loud mowers and bright lights
the smell of cut grass, gasoline and gravity
pulling at me
my open mouth gasping for rest
my roused rax around the small of your naked back
my hands puckered and return to curl
parceled between the plush furnace of your legs
soft as any fire could be

perhaps i remember so vividly
because we became more than you and me
within a dream
perhaps i still am

please do not wake me

| quod spinas |

ocean foaming at the mouth
so she lay shivered
fingers and legs
crossed in algae greens
toes
cramped in damp sand
until the ribbon breaks
like past promises

i never worked a nerve to calm hers
so she stays
shivered at evenfall
to see another break, keek, blink
and sup down the sun for one

| *february* is for |

quiet moments
she's painting her nails in the sun again
something with gold in it
in the silence—
i pass my hand over the burnt coffee steam of my open
paper cup
a rhombus beam of natural light pours,
over the bunch of bananas that are bruising in their bowl
as the calendar collects the yesterdays

today we attempt at serenity
as indolent dogs lay
soft shedding on wooden floors
sleeping and dreaming and running in place
i did not hear a single bird this morning
just the click of the furnace-flame
february defrosting a first draft
: quiet moments :

| it's late my love |

my undulating embers flow
with incendiary carry
follow now the parched pout
and salivate

next to nourish the dearth of our drought mouths
ebbing evenings flow slower
as circadian comforts
[like; whisper and graze
to skin and skin again]

soon slumber sounds soft
to hold you in
the current of our body's shroud
and nothing else

and dreams fall serene
as halcyon reprieve
rings me to sleep
in peace
like a bell

goodnight

| our senescence |

early bitter
in thick of skin
now softly frosts
like bletted quince

as medlar fruit
decay, divine
is tannin toxic
raw or ripe?

now saccharine
retro-release
our mountain ash
of memory

swathed in supple
pinkish-white
a petal spry
does petal rise

we flower, fall
and burst in boil
a labored fruit
to eat the spoils

our senescence
no stops in time
we marmalade
we alkalize

...

not cursed preserve
from growth we learn
that permanence
is just a word

so sweet we are
in blooming moons
as mason jars,

become
our tombs

| liikeness |

i was never one to salt my grapefruit
nor have i held;

- a grudge longer than a promise
- my breath longer than a minute
- hands with you

some things come easier than others
like, falling;

- down the stairs
- in love
- apart

just a spoonful of sugar
for a grapefruit grown too tart

| garden variety |

does he know that he is dead?
when he sleeps like that
truant through the mewling church music
is he a child again within a dream
when he sleeps like that
chasing daises in the dark
empyrean just behind closed eyes
does he know that he is dead?

| squelch |

a pragmatic sequence of sedation
my gut takes grain as drink behests
wearing thin the days of glory
as i rest my weary head

two decades long, an inchmeal passed
my organs ache and skin has shed
the booze flows bounties, beyond my body
to untie knots in boots of lead

i gild the garden of hops and barley
weather-vaned to windy west
low hangs the fruit in unwrapped wildwood
this is where i'll build my nest

clement is caskets built in morning
for still the sun beats hot and red
to burn the barstool, break the storming
the glass half empty, i drank the rest

| it's not you |

it's not you : it's just that,
i'm starting to think of myself—
as a restless collection of cells again

my body;
the framework of fallen—
fireworks
curated from cosmic constellation
i am starting to think—
about my consciousness again

how tightly trapped this feels;
in this clumsy structure of saltwater
this cooperative of manic molecules
of vibration—
and concentrated static

it's not you : it's just that—
i am starting to panic again
starting to feel attacked
and detached and unwrapped
in a house of mirrors—

and i am sideless—
and sightless
tired and slightly frightened,
and i am doing a life sentence—

in a cell block of my own cells
an introspective hell of my own dwelling
and it's not you; i promise
its just that—
upon closer inspection
i might not even be me

| reaper in the retirement home |

dimpled dough,
stretch sagged and circled
strewn over the low of my cheek bones
this is my redacted sleep—

of night terror for slaughtered sheep
the dark horse that comes for me
i run in place,
i cannot breathe

all of my dark thoughts—
pooled into my pupils
and everyone can see

i need to stop napping on the job

| redeye |

my first thought— was sleep
tripping over laundry in the dark
on the way to peel the sheets back

ankles chained,
with scrunched up pant legs
i know that bruise— yellow now
like most things become

golden and lighter in time

elbows butterflied,
to skin my shirt from my shoulders
as a winter draft crept in through the splinters of the window
and every exposed hair,
stood to end

my second thought was—
when will my dreams,
finally leave you behind,
find something of an understudy?
or even just a note on the nightstand
this haunting
when will it end?
like most things do
like we did
like it always does
when—

just when will sleep
become a safe place again?

| bloom |

it was a bubble;
that moment
an oil slicked orb
of deep breaths from heavy chests
weightless as the feeling of first times
it was delicate
so we dare not disturb it
or try to stop it from floating past
to rest on the head of a budding bellflower
and burst to become as it always was

| trick candles |

if my body is a temple,
than it is also a church on fire
my bones—
made from birthday candles and bad habits
and every morning, a bit more wax melts,
unto my coning malleable self

building out at the base
at moments i feel—
as a walking mausoleum
a marble layer cake,
in an unhappy marriage with gravity

to snuff and crumble,
at the mercy of your gales
surely to show, in gusted blow

and when i start to flicker,
and fizzle, and flounder in fickle flame
i will spark again—

in a new way

with a few tricks still up my sleeve
like a magnesium core—
and a heart quite incendiary

| crumbs |

a ritual—
of freshly baked broken bread
to reduce—
in our cheeks
fitted—
like a taught muscle to mute a horn
in our routine repast

we dismember the day
with sharp smiles
and our stomachs fill,
as our teeth outshine our lips

delicate communion
decadent and muting
in the disassembly line
waiting to crumb

the way things make more sense—
when we taste
when we share the latter of our days
when the sun has begun—
to devour the outer sourdough

as then,
so we break—
together

as then,
so we brake,

together

| post script |

every window is now—
ajar in the house
as the evening-cool, finds its place
in the space
and onto the underside of pillows

as such melted egg—
our sun becomes
lately glazed,
 in amber and sleepy red
the summer chemicals—

post drizzle in citrus scent
a fervent bergamot
as capricious candles dance
begs a closeness—
where there is not one

begs a vice of me

to leave the afternoon—
to my afterthoughts of you
and atrophy
you remain—

as an anchor in my stomach
a storm drain—
in a home i can't quite place
a place i can't quite home

and we will know it one day—
this malignant absence
begs a vice of me ; a drink
begs my voice to speak

and we will know it one day—
a silence the size of mountains

| run rabbit |

rationing supplies
it is four thirty a.m.
where is your suitcase?

| the grass grows taller at night |

cathexis—
as a placement
into little jars,
small moving stars
flickering bright, the firefly
with small moving parts

what level of depth will be
within the night contained
and wishing well

a glittered lung,
like glass that glows
the sparkle on grass bestows

a vibrant beam, an offering
a cello plucked
a tiny wing
unfolding into forest-fire

what level of depth will be

what level of depth will it's softness show

i am one—
with slumbering sheets
before the sun comes,
to take the moons seat

the birds are still silent,
and fast asleep
nestled into,
their plush southern trees

the liminal dawn,
with its secrets to keep
i become struck,
from the sounds of the street

squealing on by,
an ambulance screams
past the asphalt,
and into my dreams

waking me quick
and all i can think
will they make it on time
or is it coming for me?

| bumbershoot afternoon |

turned timely
our yellow sweaters pill—
in the wash of autumn
weather—
in the froth of gutters spun

to float the leaves,
candy wrappers and foul feathers
—as flags tatter

my toes are twitched,
to soggy socks in dark matter
in stark laughter
and teeth chatter

pulling softly
at my lint littered lapel
dusting ornaments
as light scatters

gleaming from the tree,
put up two months—
too early
and i feel cheap

in the surreal of plastic strings
that play and twinkle
to replicate the sequence—
as lampyridae dream

as the rooftop pings
to sing—
the songs of storm
our sweaters tumble—
in the dryer
and the front yard is flooding

| viva la flor |

for e v e r y t h i n g
met by the fall of dead petal
there is; within that messy death
a solace
that the soil stay stubborn in its softness
and of it's yielding, a root replenished

where we forget ourselves
there is; within that desolation
a pause
an answer remastered within the stationary
and of it's diligent quiet : the body blooms
of psyche, soul and mind

for e v e r y t h i n g
met by the bankruptcy of benevolence
there is; within that collapse of compassion
a patience : a fertility
a philanthropy beginning to bud
and from its sprouting
with bountiful outstretched limbs
greener grew to bare the proof
of a once fallen dry dead petal
reassembled from the loam

| closer |

i want to disappear into you
into the profundity of your perfume
engulfed in reverie
as your arms swallow my shadow
i want to fall apart
into you
fall apart
into me
and once more, to be pulled back together
as one
as we

| lucida |

the grass does not stop—
at the state or county lines
does not recognize our limits
nor did the storm that took the power out

as the dark stuck to our smiles
like peanut butter
candles lit for ghost stories

that first night,
you cracked my ribs
and stared down the vacuum of my chest
plucking *'hallelujah'* with my heart strings

my floundering fish bowl of a stomach—
capsized in nervousness

all that i knew—
was that i loved you
right then—
when the light had left us
but i couldn't find the words to say it

searching in the dark

| make |

my crucible,
to posture such adorned porcelain
the pottery of your hands—
cupped in honey

a language of amber and lightness
a symmetry of felicity and soft
i could not hold a crashing sun
that would come to match your warmth

it would be just as difficult to stay unmelted

as i paste myself something framed
of papier-mâché—
a paper heart

confetti with a pulse made of love notes
and that it shreds—
all of this unsaid
and what to make of it

what to do with all of the colorful paper scraps
layer me in the tearing—
a piñata;
waiting for the wide-end of a splintered stick

the health of a hurricane,
does the painted moth make
on wings powdered with power
little flapping flood makers

with too, it's effect brought you,
a dulcet only a dream could conjure
but here in the eye, as the storm pass by
still both exist, in butterfly effect

in chaotic kismet,
in destruction and bliss
a folded wing takes flight again,
and i wonder what's coming next

|a moment of silence|

my hands;
made of sun and soil
will not hush the page,
with merely pen
the ephemera flutter between them
the unrequited ink—

spilled like sour milk
and when we are left
with only fermented lament
as wine and molded cheese—

they will drink and sing
but not of your song
and not of my meaning

and so my hands,
made of sun and soil and song and ink
will not hush, will not brief
until the pure symphony—

the swelling song– to capture
the crescendo
of love
and of loss
and of this life
is finally complete

| " i will show you fear with a handful of dust " | - T.S. Eliot

love is only food
and i am starving
an artist emaciated
empirically

49

| cycled ellipses |

spring settles now stillest
winnowed, like the night takes soft light

as before;
the year that passed and came again
lotus homed and sat
to remember—
the white flame

the same burning bright of your eyes
and so becomes the summer
warmer in its evenings
lacquered in lightning-bug tall-grass

the art of waiting is—
to remember the feeling
of something in rotation

| be kind rewind |

she said, "god speed!"
arms out with arboreal reach
such reciprocity in catching
the kissing disease

i still have knives in my lungs
and a stutter in my speech
and i'd do it all again
and i hope that so would she

| driving drunk down memory lane |

last call
and my thoughts idle
blind and swinging—
my key-ring 'round the grip of my index

a black tab-book rests, like a calm cliff-hanger
off the edge of the neon lit bar-top
my receipt of defeat,
stuck to the wet circle of my drink

i close out with a maxed credit card
and make a stumbling appearance to the men's room
sick and hunched over,
dizzy and speaking in cursive

i am driving drunk down memory lane
and i haven't quite drank you away

i swerved into the stall and started making a call
 five rings and then voicemail, so i left one
something i will definitely regret
when i wake up tomorrow afternoon

| what nourishes me, destroys me |

i'm writing about flowers again
the tender metaphor that is;
us; as the petals of buxom bulbs
bursting something spectacular

what nourishes me, destroys me

and so it must be;
temporary and beautiful

[quod me nutrit, me destruit]

| chondromalacia |

my socks are;
dog-eared : at the toes
paper thin : at the heal
cotton stripped
frayed : habitually : mostly

considering : my affinity
for false starts : and off beats
so curs•ed be : the penalties
i am jumping in : with both feet

always : so desperate : to dive in
to dislocate my joints : to rearrange :
these frequented and freshly wet ventricles
to give you : my unabridged heart

my tongue : a peninsula : in a sea of poetry
take me : as taxidermy : as muscle memory

to leap : from the cliffs of your lips
a helical plummet : to propel
from was : to is :
to maybe again
but better this time
and much, much more of it

| ipecac |

before the storm
my bones float—
in brackish bath
fogged, like cataracts

in southeastern swamp
my limbs cloud the color
before the thunder

as i tread in my bloodletting
elegant, like red jellies

i surface like turnips
my breath return with a single word

ipecac

as now before the purge
i swallow the sea
to push down every feeling

i a m s a l i n i t y

and the tide is coming

| anoche |

in lagging late spent post unyoked
we became, a catacomb
our bed of dead, late lovers moan
in paused parade of living bones

and with our drift, it's still unknown
whether love be life, or death its role
baroque i know, it may be both
but still the cause to try once more

| life insurance |

everything i do
everything i have ever done
in this one-horse, jerkwater, pocket-sized life
has been—
to be
the tallest breath i can be
to be a legacy of lungs
spoken from the sleeve
a memorable speck
better than yesterday

for the sole purpose
of savoring—
the few fleeting seconds
of pillowed composure
without a single regret

as a wink of weightlessness—
upon my death bed

| cost efficient |

in penury proper
the wake is always ready to remind
of monetary spectacle
versus navigated sight

then bursts the exhale open
onto blue frosted grass of glass
a fog hangs low on open toes
i am barefoot in the yard out back

in the morn that favors silent trees
drops of dew dare blades to curl
as the cat lay curved with chin to knees
and webs of spiders have unfurled

expelled in smoke and coffee steam
a dovish day is at my lips
no work today, the birds don't sing
my sweater sleeves, swallow my limbs

without my name on anything
the day came cheaply still
when presence is the cost to be
and nature is the pill

this monetary spectacle
a hearse will surely hasten
i sit and smile in penury
measuring worth by breaths i've taken

| sugar and vinegar |

in the muffled snap of ripping roots
we gut our harvest from the earth
sugar beets, onion, ginger and purple carrots
yanked up like a rotten tooth

bunched and tossed into a rusty barrow
shaking off the cool caked dirt
pivoting— as i pulled and plucked
critters frenzied down below

as the sun moved past, the fresh turned soil
i met you with mason jars
we sliced and chopped the autumn haul
as you'd bring the water to a boil

a first attempt as pickling beginners
with sugar, zest, spice and vinegar
and so we pickled the better of our spoils
and then we pickled some more of our livers

| blurry |

where has your face gone?
flashed before the fireplace
wandered
sat on the floor : brooding with houndstooth

the chairs catching behind of your leftover light
that mellow roar
of shadowy jagged
crystal prisms danced from your glass
is it leather that catches your back?

arms bowed to knees, raw and leaned
wool spun round your shoulder-blades
i look and sulk in the silk you've weaved

where has it gone?
the moment
the woman that made the moon out of a molehill
where has the moon gone?
where has the time gone?
where has your face gone?

| silt |

the muddy grass path
before the hidden creek bed
was forged with bare-feet

61

| if i die before i wake |

as bohemian ritual—
in makeshift temple
beneath the wheel well
my paisley gestates

with gypsy blood—
the colour of rust
on carriage made,
from sun-burnt dust
i lay in wait—

to imbibe the weathered licks of traveled tongues
and with every word, we grow to run

bartering stories for beer
see—
this is when home becomes
in tale and memory
to trade a tease from the cemetery—

so now i lay me down to sleep
as the windows sweat
i can rest in peace
and if i die, before i wake
at least i could finally be—

 free

| we were incendiary |

dwell damp the silken puddled page
drip to ripple quiver
as loose-leaf bloats in mascara black
diluting first truths

like;
forever
& alive

to dry cracked and blank and burnt
as sullen brow in leather bound

the first love letter
written
on flash-paper

| nest: nestle |

settle down : sweet neighbor
with heated breath and subtle kiss
the lawn has grown : pushed past my knees
the weather-vane twirls like my limbs

settle now : sweet neighbor
my something old : is making fists
subtle spun newspaper
i'll bring the tea as alchemist

kettle's on : sweet neighbor
agave spun and slow to drip
settle down : homemaker
two cups of leaves & boiled twigs

settle down : sweet neighbor
a beauty's born on nights like this
temper our behavior
and leave the crystal to our lips

| death sells |

ask of three truths:
sex,
death
and plastic

after all, we are not but, walking water capsules
littered with hopeful bones and spurious holy masters;
bastard!
wasn't he?
yes see;

sex is something you have
and love is something you make
so why are we all dying
for just a chance to procreate

| ouroboros |

it was summer
the evening; dark blue and stark naked
i joined friends at a traveling festival of sorts
it smelled of smoked meats and petrichor
i pet the dew with the under of my forearms
as i lay beneath the view
the drunks began to seep from the woodworks
as dusk approached and the children went home
i too, basking in the brine

my nomadic bones pulled me into a poorly lit tent with a
muddy grass floor
there, a wrinkled old woman sat silently
she spoke softly in a *romanian* tongue
she reached for my hand and began to scan the whorls of
my grip
the hair on my neck raised as she sat without a word
just kept brushing the curved path of my future apex and
wains
she looked at me dead in the eyes
staring into my soul
somehow i understood her in the glint of her gaze
we both stared silently within the flicker of flame

she then slowly let my hand down
and blew out the single candle that would illuminate this
make-shift tent
i wanted to ask so many questions
she just nodded and smiled out of the corner of her mouth
i then kindly paid her and quietly left

my friends were still at the beer stand, i joined them as they
punched each other's arms and called each other pussies
they asked me where i had been
i told them that i had seen a fortune teller
they laughed and asked what my fortune was

i vexedly replied,
"i don't know"

they went back to their drunken pissing contests
and i just stared at the stars
i had another beer and went home

i suppose the fortune is in my own silence
in my gratitude
from time to time,
i will think of her and stop to look around myself
to see my fortune

i still see her eyes in the stars

| wane |

black moon, dark roasted
a glow on sabbatical
the sky closed its mouth

| shift |

weltered
so deep and half-eaten
within the clemency
of supple destruction
my juvenile

my soles roll
in timpani moan
and click quick
upon the cobblestone

i dance, in roam
in the warm wet wind
my toes crease
and pivot
the curves of the concrete
shaking before the cadence
de-veined in the salty breeze

sheltered in the fast practice of songs
before their endings
i swim in the sounds and let them carry me

weltered and willing/remembering to breathe
and dream

as i sing
and dance
and be

| possible chairs to stand on |

                [how many light-bulbs does it take
to change a persons]

a peppering lament
an albatross without egress
a soft spot on my ribs
and my favored left hip
a twist
i twist a light-bulb in
standing on a chair that gives
turning with anxious fists
a buzzing blip, the room is lit
my eyes adjust, just enough
for me
to finally see the exit

| hyperdry |

death came with supple hands
with pivot and grace
such crux to be
flirting with such despondency
as again i am, the uneasy me

writing myself in circles
painting myself into corners
a movement; like this
a mouse trap : a night cap : a road map

where to go when the blood thinners wear off
when the saline drip pulls back
oh, that trusty steed
so morose is that dark horse
where to go when the softness leaves
clutching an amulet in the ambulance
down on my knees
and i am all out of prayers
and we are all out of whiskey

| a toast |

my morning cup is inundated with understatements
equal parts; black coffee kisses
 & something missing
swirling between a spoon of sugar and sleep deprivation
and caffeine always makes me anxious
if distance were a drink
my cup runneth over

| how to spell colo[u]rs |

in divine staring contest
with two irises like a nebula web
the purples pursed in gold and green and blue
bled from the chaotic black : like your shadow

and mine; an umbra made of night
dusted with light as bursting bolide
on infinity and letting go
our vibrations moved like opened doors

with an ear to the earth and head in a hole
i am waiting
for that thickened thump
for that sudden blundering thundering bump,
for that sudden abrupt,

for that moment the door that led to 'us'
is so quick to slam itself shut

| off-brand batteries |

discovered now in great divide
i ask the clock to change its mind
to more a short and managed stride
ephemeral as [*irish-goodbyes*]

and the clock just keeps on it's metronome
as no, not so, as though, not yet, so stead

i stare at the ceiling, my popcorn sky
counting the ticks and blinking eyes
the smell of rain, my maritime
i swallow air just like my pride

to drown in the winds of wisteria
glitching gums spat solemn myriads
to know the holds on time is curious
to change its space, to unwind weariness

i took the batteries out of the clock
just to see if the calendar would even notice

| hyperloss |

i've got chain-mail for blood cells
minding my own business
until i am caught
entertaining fluid truths like they will dry level
but it never does

i can convince myself of just about anything
now if i could just convince myself to get out of bed
like, for no other reason than to make myself eggs
but, i'd rather cook for you instead

solder together some beautiful metals
to protect my heart and head
like, trying to love yourself
is more tangible than death

i don't much like my hairline
it's receding
like the bricks i've paved to bury my meanings
and i gave you one each day
one by one
until clean was the slate
and now i'm open and afraid
naked and shaved : exposed

because it's cold to be free
it's a warm kind of freezing
just to love me for me

| partner in crying |

today we lay under blankets
in *dark-rooms*
trying to develop new ways to smile at the sun
when the light just feels, like a cancerous courier
in our fight or flight, we tend to run

teetering unbalanced in our hypothalamus
now stronger still, with thickened callouses

pick pocketing primrose
from the petticoat of modern day [*bastet*]
to place in a vase, next to our blanket buried bed
my bouldered shoulders rests your weary head

and tears
for my partner in crying
my darling dear

as all things
this too shall pass
and i will be here
for as long as it lasts

| rearview |

if i keep cutting away at the fat—
white nuggets of the past

might i be limber enough to walk in to today?
will purpose then find me
in that strange window of a soul?

| flesh of my flesh |

hands make good cups, in baptismal blood
we returned holy water through soggy skin
as the separation poured, like a biblical flood

an obituary folded to float,
now sinks alone as a newspaper boat
inked on the river quit
and i did
run and quit and spit to spite the river quick
hands make good prayer when folded properly
but when they are open
what will be held?

| speakeasily |

gums that bleed
champagne pink
in florescent
bathroom sinks

i white knuckle through *wednesday*

sweating bullets'
bourbon drink
to slow my thoughts
my pulp and ink

as my mind might be somewhat gone now
but you should see my liver

| battle of the bedsheets |

uppercut my windows shut
coffee black and brazen sun
phonetic pälms, neath pillows clutched
audible in, my clasp and brush

my bed of sweat, my dancing dust
to wash my hands in golden cup
to move the sheets that will not budge
the day to break my sleeping drug

to force my blinds where shadows hung
to breathe into, my daylight lungs
and i must wake, for day has come
as i must go, where summer's sprung

| flash in a pan |

venerable shadow
stretch out,
with your pliable mask of midnight
to find the dust in clocks
to homogenize

within the sum of cut corners
in strengthened task
of time lapsed
as the street lights ask back in amber
our venerable shadows collect

| every so |

often
you will cross my mind
still sputter in my stomach
old gas guzzled clunker
losing myself in the hunger

every so often

| trailblazer |

self preservation; has kept me
 in a single bed
spent the winter half jaundiced
 with double vision
in the garden without gloves
the liquor store without sleep

the carnage of my ascension
on bloodied knees; has kept me
a kneeling collection of bruises
i am painting the roses red
 in a single bed
i am painting the roses red

burning the weeds for the garden
if only i didn't have to lose you in the process

|mouth full of mud|

last night got out of hand
all the swallowed bottles wallowing in the hallway
and i followed

sipping and sinking into the sea of dreams
funny the way that has always seemed to be
the answer to my wondering
like the soft of your palms and my blundering

oh sleep, my dearest lover
quiescent i have become
to reminisce in the already happened
and the maybes

and sleep and sleep and dream
and i awoke at four thirty a.m.
and trembling

| light-weight worries |

the wood pile is getting low
what bridge will be next?

a redux and woolgathering
life fixed—
on a conveyor belt
lead circles to be
and guts to rip ripely

like brown moving-boxes collapse—
when emptied

circle
takes
the square

the dumpster now encumbered
with cardboard and cares

| dollar general: wine and soap |

is this vulnerability?
a solitude i should not be romanticizing
drinking for three with ' *father john misty* '
you had a baby on the way, that never came to be
and i am getting older, whatever that means
if only i could sleep without the dark parts of dreams
is this vulnerability?
is this maturity?
or just another endless attempt
that i make to stay clean

| finds you well |

leafing through the back pages
of the *blue ridge mountains*
where the deep green mouth of *kudzu*
had swallowed the highway whole
where yellow lines and speed limits digest
in the unrest of the distant cities
where things forget their beginnings

such a desirable retirement
for my tired body
i can't shake the sensation
the urge to become immured
in this shaded coiling cascade
and let my appendages exist
within the index of tepid summer rain

call it a prologue, or something like a package
a breadth of overslept trees
bury me here
deep beneath the green
where life takes turns
just like a *kudzu* leaf

| forever young |

maybe we will eat—
from the mouth of my memory
a toothless thing, a lunacy
my thoughts are now, a spilling drink
a little hurricane, circling the drain

maybe we will pull;
from the golden cups of borrowed gods
bottomless; with clenched fists
knuckles pearled, under paper skin
with the airlessness of an oyster's grip

to fill ourselves
bathing in the estuaries
until our reflections are of god as well

maybe this time is different
maybe it takes a village
might we become the ocean
little hurricanes, circling the sea

| freckles on the window |

i am galvanized in yellow lights
to spend, within the brief of sun on your face
wild of thingness, the deepness
the elegance of your existence

a plum,
soft spots and all
you are a lullabied hum

fair of breath, pulled from my chest
something i miss, that hasn't yet left
you are the bookmarked place,
on my favorite page
you are the petrichor scent, right after it rains

you are electric, earnestly splendid
and i meant it, every word i'd say
and i will and i do, write of you everyday
as the dew starts to form
& the sun starts to fade

i am galvanized in yellow lights
and i wouldn't have it
any : other : way

my love is like a library
and i saved you a page

lest we forget maps
whereas we have in the past
as not to find my tongue split
or shackled to the ring-tops of half-empty beer cans

i cannot hold my lungs the way i used to
they rest wheezing with crackled laughs
pierced with pinholes from dream-board thumb-tacks

the tension could lay you down warm in its thickness
such is honey before harvest
nectar before nest

i am
always too quick to stick
to roads far too eroded
my glove-box is brimmed
with pages tacked of viscid fingerprints
my thumbs curved crooked to hitch

lest we forget to wear sunblock
and shoot from the hip
lest we forget
or destined to repeat it

harrowing is the pineapple rind
the wet husk,
that sat atop the compost for weeks
rotting in practiced absence
could we all be so sweet,
 on the inside of our spikes?
hollowed
gutted, gored
even the sun takes a bite
and might a fruit bloom? say, possibly two?
or will only our armored harmonies,
be left to leather,
for the flies

| 1986 |

agued in atonement
flogged in flask
a merited musk
a musty map
bead and break
my breath and back
pressed the poultice
to cranial cracks
a muster of memory
from future's past
staunch the still
and still i laugh
in familial frenzy
corrosive tact
to bleed in blunder
a stranger matched
viva voce
carapace for mask
back to the board
indelible grasp
so bristle, i work
porous pen traps
merited mediation
my moniker lapse
marry the merry
to fill in the gaps
so still i sit
to carve a new track
this light lingers lucid
and time moves too fast

| travel plans |

we were never supposed to get this old
body turned to soft churned butter
fair, feckless and calcium deficient
t h i r t y   s o m e t h i n g or other numbers

well seasoned in bereavement
& how many times
have we washed ourselves?
how many hairs will find the brush in clumps

my present indefinite temperament
a controlled burn
an enkindling rendered to mildy-wild
some kind of expired dynamite
not quite fizzled out

we were never supposed to get this old
as i am still wife and childless, but i like it
ninety-seven percent of the time
i cannot package this into two lines
l i f e
was late nights,
bloodied at hardxcore shows
now weekend trips to *lowes* & *home depot*

plastic on the furniture
playing cards in their case
powdered milk, honey, hard liquor and achievements
at the back of the spice rack
on a shelf too high to reach them

mother earth turned as we were sleeping
we were never supposed to get this old
or so the story goes
but here we are, so where shall we go?

| we are not a glum lot |

it is *tuesday* evening
the golden hour
right before the sun cuts the skyline in half
like a *gallagher* act
smashing pink mist across the clouds

it is tuesday evening
and the neighbor is cutting the grass
i'm on my way back
from a meeting
the kind that helps from drinking
as i drive past the freshly lawn hacked
the sappy sliced sod is blasting me into the past

a nostalgic lapse, of green lawns, laughs
and zero issues with abusing substances
and i chuckle under my chin,
oh what a gaffe
because i know that those days are here
again,
but i just have to know the difference
and i have to remain on track

| room & body |

a rented temple
no refund for damages
time came to clean house

| eggdrop sunspots |

a scoff of sun
peer still— in alpenglow
that tickled peak gleam
and in-between, of valley low

find i—
in belfry high
as burst the beat
of church bells toll

the cut glimmered guts
in coral tones
mark me a gaze
in floral notes

i am rock, yes i am stone
move mountainous curves
kintsugi gold
filtered gilt, upon the snow
and warm in light like winter coats

| photogenic |

womb of winter : cocooned in white
my arms shovel the fresh snow in angel angles
arched and waving
quiet night : stay silent
as the more i learn to listen ; the more i might—

hear...

slowly 'til spring let's the drowning become daises
the iced over mailboxes will crack at their hinges
packed with postcards from the other side
where you learned to skip rocks in a new language
where the sun was busier and the leaves were still spry

the greatest faith : that the next turn will come full circle
and i will be patient, making snow angels
waiting for the postal worker
to take my *polaroids*
to the other side,
where the sun has been busier
to the place you learned to skip rocks
in a different language

| water resistant |

it started with a window
an afternoon overcast in clamoring riposte
of rain on pane
i'm wide-awake again

watching the toast burn
as i'd find your hair in my sweatshirts
i saw love muddy to a dirty word

- don't get caught with passion -
is something i've learned

- don't get caught -
i tell myself,
in the white noise of the tin-trailer-roof

through the waterfall of window
i don't see a calm after the storm

| bargain sale |

collect me,

lined into your bric-a-brac fever
retrofit of trinket kitsch
a pregnant mantle of dusty cedar
sequential sate, anthologist
full-moon new in citrus cloth
grind the hooves to fix my cracks
parceled next to treasure what
something like, a woman's trash

collect me, i am
discontinued

| cold feet |

sooty sheep skulk in silent dance
upon the dimples of *big sleep's* cheek
each night a new epoch feat
a meet-cute with a curtain call

and i wear wool socks to dream
for the reaper kisses with frosty teeth
nibbling
a tango with *death's* angel

in mirthless midnight
when linear life feels like it just might be
something of a long con
i recite their count as playful songs

and i wear wool socks to sleep
to counter the cold of my frozen feet
and there, just before my thoughts retreat
is she, sweet grim of grim
sweet dreams

| hyperdeath |

great art comes with a toe-tag
it is painted with shovels
with blood and soil
it is *danse macabre*

it is swallowing static
digesting the dark
it is grizzled gut
it is brittle cough

digging depth
to hyperdeath

it is lasting awe

it is made of your muscle
it is ripped from your jaw
it eventually eats you
'til your bones become raw

great art comes with a toe-tag

and it never stops

| savor |

i know that the curtains have changed their shape
as did the place in which they'd hang
i know this bitter gift
given within my grand tarriance
my greatest hits:

sometimes it was the hospital,
other times, the airport
my leaving : stumbling into my seating
tumbling my thumbs over themselves
like a bingo-hall-ball-basket : cranking and spinning
like a dryer, beating up a pair of boots
clunking, inside it's round mechanical room
always dreaming down from my small window's view

my foot : pedaling marathons on my knee
unsure of where my legs should be
as my heart would hang by a thread
a few strings left inside my chest
i know the silent way people become less,
remembered : or thought about

the way perception brings new lessons
when the plane takes off
the way we become specks : ants on a quilted blanket
the way heavy doesn't seem like so much anymore
but i still remember you : a picnic
ants on a quilted blanket
and all the sweet things that brought them there

| poetry vs pottery |

a prayer like porcelain
how it would sound to break
that capricious kind of fragile
in every clanking cracking shattered scrape

now: a ghostly absence of dust
a darker stain on the wood from which it lain

i would blame it on the cat if i had one

| two acres of forest, and an above ground pool with tree
branches in it |

i stir the glass with my finger
swirling; clanking; the ice-cubes sing
like wind-chimes
i lick and flick the drips from my index

burning—
a coil of citronella
as a collection of insects wage their war
upon my exposed ankles and soft neck

this will be—
a muddy summer of blood shed
yet the quench—
from the freshly blended refreshments
 —seemingly remits

| *cloudland, az* |

it isn't : somehow : gone
no, the road did not take it from me
did not seem to bury the lead
in every malleable mile of endless desert
after everything : it isn't : somehow : gone
    that feeling

in all of those sideways ridges,
waving and drifting
tiny little brittle crystals,
sanding and gritting
in the dereliction of dustbowl wind
the vestiges of highway signs,
flail and unlace like a tattered sail

yet, in that brazen grainy bleach of a breeze
it is : still not : some how gone

no;
no matter how golden that road puddled
on the first flat pause of the horizon
no matter how honey bright the light could come to blind
she was still there : is still there
my love : in the sweetest of shinning aureate

still there
in my favorite memory
my favorite time : to surrender
unto the torrid desert shelving,
however intimate or unknown

| sleep away |

soft water from the sink
my books of borrowed time
you were my bursting kernel
of truth in every lie

my night-shaded nightcap
tonight i'll sleep outside
below the wishing welkins'
moon pulling at my tide

i shiver soft and secret
as cosmic pantomime
swallow now sweet sedative
and finally close my eyes

good night, good moon, good morrow

as again, i say goodnight

| melt |

stormy city : spinning splash
and twist the tipping toes in muddied puddles
your umbrella swinging yellow
as fulcrum nunchuck

tracing crooked criss-cross
painting temporary frames
we moved in hollow color
bolder than black : faster than grey

move! move! move!
more rapid than the rain
quick! quick! quick!
'fore time catch up again

if we stop : we shall shatter

and you did
wash away
in a puddle
pareidolia

so i stare;

to still in dazing dream
your face before the drain

| the kissing disease |

my phone chimes
a *pavlovian* programming
quick to catch me in a salivated serenade

message read :
"meet me at the bodega near the *crocodile*? i miss you"

aloud: i whispered
your words into my world

it's two a.m.
and i am lost
in a fickle *freudian* cocaine concerto

message sent :
okay.

cut to the must, of *seattle* alleys
we sat under the wet
where the cobble stone and asphalt met
we kissed once more for the final time

and i've been sick to death ever since

| timber |

we move now; like late autumn
silent limbs in halt; a potential woodpile
and un-held, and fast dead
stoic and golden and wet
browning and bronze
and deep caliginous red

without rustle or gutter or breath
the soon of forenoon — a morn
-break : a ladle of azure and milk skimmed
a frigid drip, to borrow and dip
from the blackwater midnight's brim
and we layer the heavy cloth to our skin
within its silhouette

we sit still; like empty churches
waiting for sunday;
for the bigly blood draw
and the open sky of *november*
waiting for the body to catch up
for the fresh grapes to paint our tongues

but we do not kiss
but we do not speak;
of yesterday or growing old together
our leaves to spin in leisurely loosen
slacked to tatter
from our honeymoon green

as pestilence waits in the pause

...

we move now; like late autumn
and we do not kiss
we do not hold our bodies like the summer
not towards each other

but to a frosty fog of the long forgotten
as timbering tinder
as dusty oaks, come winter coats
with far more bark than bite
with far more choke than throat

| tenebrism |

frederick barnard offered,
that "a picture is worth a thousand words",
so surely it would be,
that you are a flickering silent movie
playing on repeat

| seppuku |

there are buzzards hovering above my bed
the sliest bastard scavengers
they gawk & leer at my slowing neck
soliciting my skeleton

my pine for you is palpable
this peckish sentiment;
this empty chest; an un-patched pothole
a pallid-white drum stretched

my ache for you is audible
stentorian and quenchless
of heaven sent and long since left
tempestuous and breathless

a razor blade like ringing,
in disquieting lament
it sounds now like a dinner bell
for the buzzards and all their friends

| night sweats |

never forget—
how rail-thin that room became
emaciated : ribs showing : a needle-head

old furnishings, reduced to matted marks in the carpet
barred shadows through the blinds
never eating; except for the light

when the sun emptied itself
i emptied myself there too

firstly, my thirsty heart,
withdrawn and fell out
still beating to the dripping riddles of lovers tongues
sharp to speak

a chain of cigarettes lancing my lungs
and my skin; a shivering swamp
a fever that refused to break with the dawn

night sweats

then it was my stomach,
made of *death's head hawk moths*
flapping with their skully-backs
wrenching every gear in my gut to glass
ground finer still to hourglass sand

l o s i n g   t i m e

the liquor too, slowly sowing it's sickness;
undoing the laces in my shoes
loosening every tooth, that smiled for you

...

finally my mind, of it's cluttered ruckus
it's utter numbness, a dumbness

in the black mass of a relapse
i don't ever want to go back

the madness, on the edge of a breath
i don't ever want to go back
i don't ever want to go back

| bones & dominoes |

etching my thumbs into the crumbs of my styrofoam cup
i am at a meeting bleeding
and we all talk about what we should of done
we are dumb;

and blank
and trying to salvage some face
like dominoes, we race; looking to fit an empty space
a matching place, clear the board and clean the slate

like clean would somehow change everything

but i am still numb,
just differently undone
and this time
i can really feel the empty white light come

bones snapping together to add up to none
like snake eyes would have a better sum
below three and you're out of luck
like all the wins were not enough

and my plastic canvas, these textured anvils
a double blank saved, until the end
to guarantee no points will be lost
no points can descend
and i wrote all of this with dirt underneath my fingernails

i guess i'm not so clean after all

| love vs lexapro |

not late of any fight, left within my blood
old wounds reopened;
to re-edit; to re-graft; to re-scar
but love does not bury in the dead
does not a fly welcome it's landing,
as desiccated leather

this labor of harrowed heart
an energy of memory
love recycles, it reanimates in the open air
it moves above headstones
above bed frames
and to breathe it again,
could i still find it in my lungs
to re-inflate this vacant vessel
the steadfast pull, to rip me up and out
from these stubborn and sleepless sheets

| clear daughter of the stars |

to fill from the heavens, one must follow the rain
i will listen for love where it lives
the throat of a songbird, in the *shenandoah*
i will still myself there
as a vibration in the vista

i will let the last of my body heat,
draw from my bare feet
as the soft wet soil, pulls me down

with squalid skin, i will build
i will burn bivouacs
as retreat
and let the flames push camp further out every week

and i will still myself in the song
i will be still, i will be fire

a roaming home

a vibration of vivification
a dram of the promise land
i will taste the sweet water,
and still in the songs of the *shenandoah*

| how to avoid eye contact |

tree nuts fall from on high : a meteor shower
of plummeting acorns : still green
i am caught in between;
the sun and the shadow of a squirrel
nibbling the air
it's fluffed thick-bristled tail
spasms; a distraction : a magicians trick
the last thing you'll catch
is the back burning dust
wafted; into the ghost trail
of where it perched prior for five seconds
before their disappearing act—
became all curtains

| i write with more pause now, as if i have already written
my entire experience of existence into extinction |

when i was a much smaller collection
of skin, bones and blood
one mid-nineties afternoon, at my school friend's parent's
house, i was messing around on their dusty upright piano
that sat sunken in the corner of their family room.

i didn't know how to play, so i just punched a bunch of keys
at once in a left to right progression. whilst pretending to be
elton john or queen or whatever, i turned my head,

to receive positive affirmation from my chuckling buddy. all
the while with my hyperactive hammering, i had loosened the
lid to the keys, causing it to drop down, fast and heavy onto
my skinny little hands.

twackk! gurrumptchhdjinggg!

this was one of the first times i desperately wanted to cry
but couldn't, not in-front of my friend. just had to shake it off
while using the few curse words that my elementary school
vocab had acquired

there are moments, that i will still reflect on that internalizing
experience
and the stumbled sound of d minor under knuckles crunching

as if that isn't exactly what i am still incessantly attempting

breaking myself daily, to find the perfect chord
the perfect sad note that would summon the lord,
or something

...

it's been a while since i've sung out loud
even alone in the car
and i don't fully remember many lyrics anymore

that deafening pain, still holds a place
in my routine of diurnal journals to this very day
something about wanting to scream and cry
so loud that it would shatter the plates,
but no one wants to hear it or bother
with why you are screaming in the first place

| a pound of flesh |

a teaspoon of honey
glazed in gold, fruits of flower
snails to the end of the silver spoon
pouring steamed milk into lavender cups *made in china*

as *chamomile* and lattice,
mingle in the dour of day
it looks like rain
as *the belladonna* is calling from the shade
a whimper
the stale of subtle plague

to have my cake
a pound of carrot
to eat my cake
a pound of flesh

to lay in dewy grass of double chin
as we are martyred before the garden

to channel the soil and inherit the soul
to give up *arcadia* and rest in the mud
to bury ones pride to colour the bloom
grass is greener equated with blood

a pound of flesh
for an ounce of love

| kept |

how things become commonplace:

a hair brush, a displaced button,
a sepia-toned photo on the bureau
a tan line from your wedding ring
the sound of sirens, and heartbreak

the commonality; like creature comforts
like privacy
grow thin and used and obsolete

just sepia-toned
and old

something new is:

washing my hair for once
and loving your children like they were my own

i am not sure what space is now
but i don't really want to know

| i want to grow a garden |

i want to grow a garden
i want to grow a garden and measure time by the shadows
that stretch from the soles of my feet and bare toes
i want to pull wild rhubarb and chew its sour stalk
until my mouth runs dry
with the summer sun on my neck
and the mist of fresh rain moving through the humid air

i want to run my fingers through thick blades of blue grass
as the man on the old wooden stage shreds his banjo
i want to watch the lights go out and stare out at the
silhouettes of families on the hill
into the *july* sky,
as the fireworks explode into a pyrotechnic song

i want to feel
i want to feel free again

i want the sounds of crickets and screen doors chirping and
creaking as we tell stories on the porch
with fire flies and rocking chairs, softly swaying back and
forth into the hours of sunsets

i want to grow a garden
and pick wild raspberries
i want to smash them into my cheeks until my belly is content
and my hands are riddled with crimson sticky stains

i want to be free
i want to grow a garden

| snail mail |

it starts with fingerprints
i try to leave them everywhere—
i can
like postage sent—
to strange cities
an invisible place holder
for when i come back again

and i was—
doing something really important in the rain

but will any of this even count
if it is to all become washed away?

| hyperglass |

that secret place beneath the pillow
where fear undulates
where sweat and tears and sand
crystallize in your sleep

a science of silence
and snore
collecting every breath a body can bare to hold

what am i

a man, a martyr of memory, a mollusk
always waking
in the wrong place
the wrong room
the wrong arms
the wrong face
in the wrong mirrored bathroom

a body,
that is not my own
a prison of my own making
a prisoner
of my own unconscious creation

| the sound of your car
        leaving the driveway for the last time |

vacuous gurgle
an onomatopoeia
for two hearts, bled out

| curl |

the morning ran ill,
in our late and sun blocked room
with sheets that were built for winter
and so they wore warm and weighted,
over my naked collar bone and shoulders
gripped across my ear and eyes

and time had seemed to pass between weeks,
instead of nights

always waking to a half empty closet
a make-up-less bathroom
no hair dryer on the floor,
or rumpled panties by the shower mat

i haven't cleaned the powder residue from the vanity
and the toothpaste spittle—
is still on the facet knobs and mirror

this can't be
can it?
no calls, no loud laughs stumbling in at three a.m.
no breakfast to make
for anyone
anymore

just a carpeted-to-hardwood barefoot tread,
from the bed to the fridge
staring at condiments and beer
where did that chocolate-cherry birthday cake run off to?
did i eat it?
i don't even like cake
but it was the last leftover thing to touch our mouths

washing myself in the sink, every couple of days
as lately i don't really see a point to change
...

everything i did
was for

      you

aren't here

was

blueberry pancakes for the girls
with sprinkles
and i am lost in water and batter
and questions
and glitter
and you aren't here

| cloudburst |

the tilt of your head;
moved like a swiveled bear trap,
canted back to catch the big rain
a storm has come to wash the sordid city
warm and fast;
as the swollen ocean
guts the sky

a filament flared and a teeth rested
designed over your bottom lip
like dovetails, fluttered together
and every muscle;
kept your skinny laugh clever between them

to keep more inside, and out and away
behind those pearly whites; there is a hardware
to the reservoir of cloudburst
before those pearly gates,
there is a great flooding

| micropolis |

the bulb is for the blossom
but wilt she did receive
some petals on the pillow
of sleep and withering

| footloose |

maybe we are;
just the groundskeepers
just the after-burn
of a galaxy already collapsed

not but some garish ghosts
adorned in guardrails
bending and meeting,
on a pre-spun spindle
floating and weaving,

through the worlds of old
the music : the kaleidoscope
and maybe when the record skips
we will remember;
the stars that held our tongues
the heat that burned our lungs

and oh, might we come to finally find
that complementary rhythm : to be
and soles, souls, soles, souls, soles
dancing : stampeding
tamping : re-kneading
our impressions :
sleeping : yet not dreaming
but remembering

yes, maybe we are just memorizing
    the foot work
to the path : the music : the kaleidoscope
a mile a minute : completing
our impressions : our ceremonies

...

through every bath of sound
every déjà vu
every puzzle pieced mosaic
through every inchoative colour
of a preliminary after-life

| soft tissue |

my cells release what's left of us
scrubbing at, the rust and dust
the bunnies 'neath, my bed-shaped-crutch
and soap-scum tarried the off-white tub

i lay in the walls of my brickwork
dividing whats left of our pictures
the sleeping wolf outside my door
as i decode in my favorite elixirs

i scrub my skin, until it bleeds
to wash you off and far from me
our love is now a cloth of bleach
there's nothing left here underneath—

that lonely little microscope
i try to zoom and find some hope
there's nothing left to see here now
just sterile skin and empty bones

| pull |

today was a wet dog
shaking off its soaking mud-coat—
in the dove-white hallway

it seems, clean is for the birds
and i am just a clay pigeon
trying to maintain my pottery

| idle thoughts |

my heaviest permanent,
is in the rot of snail
the slow squish of my squirming thought
nightly wander, in glittery mucus
a muted gold
a reminder
idling in my masochistic memory
and when the shine strikes,
the shadows will sharpen their teeth
and turn my thoughts turbulently
to rest in the jest of mumbling mania
and alcohol
and piano
and pillow talk
so i lay and rot and shine and drink
and you trail the glittered pillow
and so we squirm in the latter of our promises
and so we turn our backs as we turn off the light

| take my eyes with a melon baller |

this hunger's becoming a habit
it stirs in my stomach and plays in the acid
like the worms would flirt in a casket
it straightens me snug and buckles my jacket

it's always behind me in private
it's tortured as time
it's quietly violent
it chases my dreams in the silence
i can't look away
it's glued to my eyelids

i think it was born in our distance
i think it was you that was starting to miss this
luring me in with your kisses
then blinding me, signing me up for your hit list

who is more hungry for heart ache?
more willing to love or willing to break

and then i did
and now you win

covering more ground as a fucking snake

| units |

the east has caught the west
and so i become, ambidextrous
to sleep different
with cold shoulders

which side will shiver tonight?
where will i wake up
the couch

angels sing
by the skin of my teeth
posed in confession
as i silently speak

into the dark space of the living room
praying into the pillows
praying like you were sitting right there
praying like it would of meant something

| on the rocks |

it is midnight,
and i am properly maudlin—
in the middle of the bar; a weepy laugher
slamming stories on a chit spike

this is my prosthetic personality
a defaulted drunkard
impaling my problems—
on the end of a long tab

a story of leaving my body
on a bar stool, head on a swivel
eyes in a backspin

playing the only hardxcore song—
available on the jukebox
and whisper-screaming it at strangers
jumping and drumming on the backs of chairs

it used to be so easy
to fuck the world into the night,
when all that i had was time to lose
cocaine in the graffitied bathroom
it was so easy—
to leave my body

until there wasn't one left to return to

| hymn to limn |

polished of wavering whispered croon
a song that moves, flicker in, and out
the same dance as candle flash
i sing to you,
low and lightly
i sing to you,
because i have to,
because i love you

my voice is the quiet shy of feather fall
a secret song, lest spoil it all
the cadence is the key
where the song slows down in speed
and the swoon of all the crooning hearts
thereto shall surely bleed

| bathe and barter |

the milk has curdled of such a moon
tucked behind the clouds
plush and puffed to pour
as *zeus* tills the tilted welkins

torrentially

the tree-frogs bark in the black
and tonight the neighborhood cats will be fat

this whirring weather
argues at my window
snapping at the glass
the cracking lash
of every whipping branch

as the duality of my body begs
a water in my weight,
as drum and bass
stuck in place
i am now heavy as the rain

and wondering

exactly how many pounds of light,
will i need to take, to payback the sky
and zeus allusively answers
"come in, the water's fine"

| my demons, could beat up your demons |

for three days straight , i laid awake
on nicotine and coffee
and ever since the second day,
i couldn't fight these demons off me
every word i spoke to you, my love , i meant
but i couldn't help from coughing
i just want to have my cake and eat it too
i guess i'll just lick the frosting

| drug mule |

in bedlam again
a retaining wall bricked,
around white coats and white cups
with pills of blue and green and pink

i take them just to cough cleanly
and eat bologna and cheese
three times a week

with yellow mustard and yellow pills
the kitchen is filled
with nothing but sodium treats
i take the red ones to get to sleep

the purple ones, to keep-off the mean
i take them all for each reprieve
i take them, and stare and drool in dream

in bedlam again, and i asked for this retreat
four walls, with white paint and turquoise sheets
i asked for this, to keep me from me

i take them all in bedlam
and this time, i'm not sure if i'll be leaving

| equator |

my skinny sober fingers
cracked and crunched and crooked
as we lay
in cool soft palm of snappy grass
through dimming cast of passing glance
& second chance

with pointed pitch of perked-black pupils
struck and stuck to the sky in starry stare
our limbs spread and spilled
in blooming flash of frosted flares

sprawled heavy before dawn
like wet dead weight
sunken into one another
as the glutted sun begins to break

oiled and glittery and gold
to lather the soil in buttery wolds
fecund—
of many prosperous sums
our axiom of answer, from linear to one

our hands in spacial churning;
knuckles rub and work our surface
into friction fire, with burnished purpose
our frost-bitten digits, wax in perfect fervor

a sugar worthy of held tongues : a familiar
a warmth to space out : to appreciate
before blister
the sun now positioned on our pelts,
pouring without filter

...

so we slather in spf paste on paste on paste
candied skin like pearled taffy;
and taste
running rapidly roused in our stationary frames

hello, what is your name?
i will give you mine if your time has the space
for ajar is the bar as we walk with posthaste
we are called to a fate, in shared search to equate

like something to make of our pigeonholed praise
to settle our nerves and to switch off our brains
might a promise of partner: to dance and to lay
or to just find a friend with a place we can stay

| little things |

cut grass in overcast
and there
just before me
a waddling stagger in summer bare feet
and a sundress saved from the seventies
a slow stride
baby blonde leg hair moving in the slight of breeze
the little houses in regress, as i to catch up with she
i leave my presence
in a quietly content head nod
and keep walking
it's raining now
and i am happy

| pecking order |

the flutter
of one bird in the hand
a song blossomed within my palm
is worth two in the burning bush

fingers folded like a shy flower
cupping to preen a warbler beak
thumbing sweetly such fragile skull

as light as a feather
tenuous as the touch of strings
a song blossomed within my palm
is worth two in the burning bush

and let go
without hold
and sing songs of the sky
and sing songs i will, of our temporary time

| integuments |

look at all of that water
wild traveler
wanders a cloud and asks for nothing
my body heals itself the same

in my sleep, in motion, a mind of its own
a wound barricades alone : reflexively
before my cartilage : a glue of bodily fluids

look at all of that hard work
wild traveler
a stitch of scar tissue in the making
my body is a cage

and sometimes, the greatest pain,
is realized under the flush of running water
after the bacteria breaks from your blood
and the numb of initial shock wears off

| resuscitate / remain |

that singular moment
of swelling tide
when the ocean punishes the coast
parching the cliffs in post kiss
left of mossy rock and wet fingerprints

and low orange ribbons of sunset
strung across the sea
a choice between lighthouse & wave end
i wish to be,

right there
in that moment
to be painted with the rocks
and moss and shells and birds
in that moment : with you and the ocean
to be punished like a watercolor

| sweet nothings |

a sugar cube dissolves;
tiny morsel in my cheek
          breaks down
to simple syrup
          melts— into sweet nothings

like;
i would give you everything
          spoken quietly
my words
          take them
my love : take that too

i would give you everything

a sugar cube in our tea
swirling in the steam
and spinning now in unison
          like the saccharine
of you and me

| brunch on the fault lines |

fragility is:

the feeble beat of my pining heart rate
a fabergé egg, with an expiration date
a crumb cake in an earthquake
the weight of silence before it breaks
and shake

and beat that golden yoke—
until the whites no longer show
you may just make an omelette out of me yet

| doin' time [a lullaby] |

love— is a cautionary tale
i could write your story the same
with infinite inkhorn and ripe pulp
on a cold mattress in bedlam
four walls, three hots and a cot

love— is an eraser
it is white-out with the lights out
if not to draw you in dim light
than to sing you in the dark

the noise of my voice, to carry like a ghost
through bulwarks shaped like hearses
love is a counterpart[ner] in crime
it is a lesson in death, if it leaves you behind

love is senescence, it is losing your mind
love is endless and relentless
love is protection
    love— is a life sentence
and i am willing to do the time

| deracinated waves |

my roots are drunken limbs
in free-formed sew
searching : unsettled : and stumbling
waving down birds, climbing onto roofs
searching, stumbled and unsettled
waving down cabs, drying out—
needing water
passing out halfway to your house

| look god, no plans! |

i am emulsified,
of emotion and of their traps
as i practice death nightly
with a small pocket flask
and steal every answer
to questions i'm too afraid to ask

: everything infinitely temporary :

so i run on,
like un-punctuated sentences
in long breath
hapless,
but albeit happy

in the forever fall of *rome*
and sky and love
until the dust of our bones
becomes—
the foundational mud
        of our predecessors inevitable
dystopian huts

and the future generations will ask their elders,
"what if g o d
        was one of us?"

| echo location |

a guttural clatter
a death rattle my ribs
the sound of our love as an echo
in bedroom eyes and empty swimming pools

coated in waxed poetry
like;
dipping your fingers into the hot flash of candles spent

and peel

dead skin to fall with the thick flakes
a pantheon of pre-named graves
a place-keeper, all the same
as i follow the echoes that lead the way

| snatch |

nooks shook—
to cranny corner
it was under flipped mattresses—
and hidden journals
the blood that stopped
beating— of my burgled heart
a deafening quiet
and all was silent
as you scaled the terrace siding
in cat-like exit strategy

nooks shook—
to cranny corner
it was under flipped mattresses—
and hidden journals
the blood that stopped

| cancer season |

ash droops— half drawn— half written
halfway through a poem — and i am heavy
i am so tired— and ostensibly snake bitten
but i am still trying to write

the cherry of my last cigarette
sighs—
burns bright
along side
the extended hours—
of the typewriter night

of smoke ribbons
a pirouette
from the ash tray— for the overused words
—and a glass of fire
as to undress my mind

as i—
need you here
want you here
i will smoke you here
i will write you here
i will drink you here

i type—
are you here yet?

but there is no reply

| ozarks |

the night;

cast iron black with friction cricket
celestial sparks carved glinted dew
teetered the aphid on roots undone
as jaws of ivory pierced the view

densest cotton of cattails spearing
upward space in tussocks grew
muddied boots on porch's landing
acid horns with bitches brew

curtains drawn, the rivets rustled
modern man, made windows blue
washboard legs of lullaby
wooden rocker, in dampest hue

off the grid my senses sharpen
minstrels, monks and *chaplan* too
behooved to bed the books read backwards
careened the love i had for you

alone in dank, of *ozark's* chapters
crushing calms made silence new
i held your hand in marshy back-lands
i left my mark with waffled shoes

slipping grasp with humid palms
owls ask— of morning moon
endings spent in midnight pastures

to read it back

to start anew

| pocket watched |

they are paving the streets again
pot holed; bumper cobble stone
high noon reflects each invisible line
like cataracts
and the bearded men are in neon day-glow

i have a cigarette for lunch
as a sun-beaten man plays harmonica down the road
stomping the earth to a metronome like meteor crash
hair peppered with *memphis* smoke
he never asks for the time
he too, glowing invisible, like the lines in the road

despondent yet diligent
ice cubes crackling in his cup
a cigarette for lunch

besotted,
i stare and place a soundtrack to my surroundings
the orchestral hymns of garbage trucks,
guffawing through the slender side-streets
and a fusty, foul fragrance
of yesterday,
now spoiled and forgotten

they are paving the streets again

| count the droughts |

a thirst rips me straight through
my throat, parceled with hard sharp swallows
missing the morsel of your mouth
a melting mint on mine

soft chalk, white frost
a cool breath from chilled tongue
salivating satiated,
with a liquid akin to lightning
counting the seconds until the thunder
to multiply your distance
rolling in

| *june*, monsoon and union |

something small in the hallway
soft footprints
and golden braids
here we are to meet again

you touch my forehead
to kiss my skin, you catch my wind
right before i'm able to topple
all before the flood takes

what drug could this be, that we have tasted?
and you answer me with "love"
and i feel the heavy levee break
and everything's okay

| sleep on it |

the finisher : within the end of a laugh
where little teeth forget
where pillows, turn them into cold hard things
as raw gums become ellipses

salt water washed : waiting for morrow
when light speaks through a sheet
whispered over the window
my excitement; now sprightly vibrant

as joy—
called and bounced between walls
and i screamed,
oh, and i shouted out loud!
that i was visited—
by the night mouth mystic
that they had taken my tooth—
just as the fairy tale had claimed!

i still think about my body parts being turned into money

| sans aloe vera |

the textile of july;
to sit out
within its misty walls—
of sweltering southern velvet

a hot blooded ambrosia
an alchemy—
of melting—
of sweet dark greens and fat ripe peach

to sit—
in the loudness of the sun
to let it verbalize
around my neck—
above my collar bone—
as howling rose

i have always burned— so easily
as a fresh coat comes—
now every few weeks
i have always burned so easily—
it seems

for you and the weather—
in ninety degrees
and i will surely burn
so easily—
in this heat

without any *aloe vera*
to neutralize this feeling

| what would schrödinger make of sleep? |

a revolving door
of dream and reality
spun simultaneously
and we both are — and are not
here,
between the sheets

| crave |

cupboards
cup boards : meant for
the bread marbled like a cosmos
a molded space for past names
a gate : a wait : too little : too late

cupboards : my hands have been on every handle
the planks : looking for a plate
staring at the derelict of something uneaten
at midnight : i think of sweet provisions
that sugar to rush my tongue : straight to my blood

the kind that makes me want to taste you less

|cerca maria|

glory be! oh, glory be!
as never a dull point has been
or will be— found in you
as the sharp of your rosed cheek finds me too

not a heart as big— could come
to hold within my chest
could not find the space
to hold steady, such churning
such pulse of felicity
and i am made small—
outside of myself

and when i am left to the winter—
i will sit loose
i will beg of the fire—
and i will burn
i will sharpen myself on your generous flame
and i will endure the rake of ember coal
i will become whole— to the core
within— and of your everglow
as never a dull point has been
or will be—
found in you

| quietus |

within the endless petals,
an empty revel
never quite to catch up
as i attempt, to paint your perfect
pushed my pen for paper's sake

with one page now, inside the grave
and some pale dead flowers in a vase
i fear my love, to slowly become—
a quiet <u>casket</u>
      a
      n
      c
      h
      o
      r
      i
      n
      g

| white smoke |

a cornsilk pale sun
yoke of a faded daisy
it's fire season

a cornsilk pale sun
yoke of a faded daisy
it's fire season

| seeds of reverie |

make what you will
if my words fell— heavy
or sedentary
maybe dusty
maybe with my eyes closed

initials kissed—
into wet cement
a simple sort of permanence

the way that rocks form
or worlds
or how gardens become galaxies all of their own
with time and a plastic water can
my words are yours
to sew and grow

| honeysuckle headstone |

in the dark
there is a strange berry,
with bright red backing bracts
where i'd drink from the moon
in a cradle of maps

when the mountains would shake
with honeysuckle hands
black twinberry shrubs—
at the treeline would dance

in the dark
there is a black lake,
on the mountains back paths
where you'd hover with stones—
so gaily you'd laugh

no shadow would frame—
your form was too fast
as a ghost of the lake
with the moon laughing back

in the dark
there is a strange berry
in the dark
a black lake

in the dark
where we're buried
in the dark
where we stay

∞ and the waves carry on,
to an infinite place
to ripple forever,
like the mountains would shake ∞

| allergy season |

the variables of poison leaves,
bees—
and the strict scrape of pavement
a heed need be taken,
before hyperventilation

and love
and distrust
the sting before the bump

and variables—
like you,
like pavement

a heed need be taken

before it's anaphylaxis
or pain medication—
that we decide to play with

| continental breakfast |

in vesper's breath
the dry dust— of dead skin
& books
& lovers,
moves over me, as a stagnancy

suspended like a cosmos
in the ember red light
like a parliament of magpies
in hot august flight

to land—
to settle upon my suitcase
my travel sized goodbye
my "how many times?"
my vinyl stack of *bright eyes*—

filled up with the former stories
of yellow birds and better times
and so before i go,
before i leave this all behind—

i check my pockets, and check the time
i check my oil, and check the lights
i check the mirror, and start to drive
i check the sheets, on hotel nights
i checked the box for a single bed

a n d   t o n i g h t

i am not checking my phone
and i won't be saying "sleep tight "

| black widow |

knocking on death's door
an optional idiom
for asking your name

| [l]over |

coward— i was
to calm my shakes— before the sunrise
take sedatives before sleep
and drinks before breakfast

and i drank you— under the table
and out of the room— and out the house
—out of my life

yet after everything—
i still shake— and i still sedate
and i still drink
before sunrise, before breakfast
and it is disastrously derailing
how quickly quiet— everything became

| sleep paralysis |

bloated as a bell— i wake
chimed into a splitting headache
a stampeding murder of crows
crease the exits of my whimpered west cheek
prone to buckle
taught to topple
i've been building here without concrete
my stability, my foundation
has been missing now since last week

| nimbus |

within the pretense of thick rain
and dark drumming : flash flooding
as quick the lights would brightly escape the sky
humming and hovered
above the asphalt : all of those shiny streets
opalescent and gleaming

lofty overcast : expansive and vibrating
a witness, as woven and warm i'd lay
two windows : made of glass
life seems to repeat that way

to offer something so fragile and intangible
a beauty that the body breaks
i held a reflection in tiny vibrancy
and curled my body became

a vocation of observation
a sketch artist
with stories told in glancing blow
as my prehensile palms,
curved to catch
the offerings of an autumn evening down pour

shaped in half-circle : searching for
the gold in the gutters : the blue in the flume
a moiety mimicked
like the mid-waining moon

restored

| coffee & rhythm |

what clamoring the sun had made
as it beat blue, over the mountains
you were hardly a person in its blinding brilliance
observing birds
and car alarms
from our one available ear
to feel
your warm bare feet pushed against the tops of mine

as we swam,
in the resonating religion
of the work week's persistent pull
from sheets and into showers and shaved body parts
i would pull at your naval
to see if you still smelled of sweet *florida* oranges
embossing my natural baritone
into your porous ripe flesh

making ripples of songs,
to the beat of laughing children in the next room
what freeing notion
to touch the mirror and have it touch back
to look down and see a shadow
one that has taken more body
far more than before
from when the sun beat blue over the mountains

what clamorous concepts
of little clones with free thought
what cantankerous curves; a path found us in the dark
to find a drum
beating in the next room
of laughter
to find us bound

from when the sun beat blue over the mountains

| benumbed or one |

paint me in dolor colour
as melancholic shadowbox
where the dust cannot touch me
but pleasantries are out of stock

as mirth and merry make haste
but at the glass, they have been blocked
it is not what you lock out
stead what's locked in, that truly haunts

and all i want
is an unclenched jaw
this pressured pestle grinding rot
i'll purge my misanthropic thoughts
'til this stolid stubborn fucking stops

personality
a sequential reaction
to love, or lack of

| myers-briggs |

personality
a sequential reaction
to love, or lack of

| the archaeologist |

my professor, tannin spat
walked with braided legs
skin of gin, skeleton; pretzel soft
parched in herringbone tweed

house on cinder blocks
dredged from the drunken lake,
his office and bed now a rusted out *chevy*
paisley socks, pocket notepad
for too many words to remember

blanched beads shift
where his eyes should be,
a glaucous pantomime
poised now only in parchment

my mentor, of houndstooth heroism
buckled under water pressure
as my glass sings tap water songs
pitching higher as it fills to silent

a life in thistles to change young minds
weeded and greener still
a give in his sides and chin
sockets now sag, black and thin

was it cancer or candor of cantankerous kids
i wish to fix my professor's skin
my teacher, slouched austerely,
lamenting new learners

an unhinged academic
now shriveled and sedated
a dapper raisin,
a mustached denizen of mildewed page

...

i sit, in the front row
with rabid spume, i stare
to read his whispered lips
to grant his grimace one last doughy brain to deep fry

he tread through thought,
threaded thimble-less at the wharf of wet minds
a drop of blood fell, pinpricked by piers
to paint his brow upright in red

my professor, chemo spat
an archaeologist in his own right
of wool and leather
lain silk spun in oak and ember

to pass, baton of *baltimore*
torch of temperament
through black sagged sacks
he lives in light, in lieu of loss

my glass sings saltwater songs
pitching lower as swinging chariots
though not quite the most pious flight
the wind prods the haymaker

and i,
a secular scorch
in his knotted pine pipe
my professor entered the big sleep,
and dream, my teach'
i bid you to rest in peace
farewell, goodnight and goodbye

| exhibition |

a sober oyster
cloistered into the corners of crafted company
a manifesto read
do not touch the art

drunk and sunken
self fulfilling gumption
burning *monet,* to clear any impressions
do not touch their heart

hungover headache
panic and pulsing
i slammed one back
to wash it away
do not touch me

| bottom shelf |

i am in a constant custody battle with my brain
poison. poison. poison. poison. poison.
obsession
do not move the oven knobs
this is hush money
a brown bag special
addiction. addiction. addiction.
tricking my tongue again
a master of deception
turn. turn. turn. turn.
turn off the oven.

a blackened caught-fish
i am cooked and caught in smoke
smoke. smoke. smoke. smoke. smoke.
a caged bird without a song
tarred & de-feathered
lucky plucked
plucked. plucked. plucked. plucked.
fuck.
turn off the oven
oven. oven. oven. oven. oven. oven. oven. oven.

shucks. shucked.

drunk

| lucky loosies |

tobacco rolling in my fingers
kettle heats up to a hiss
pull it from the blood-orange burner
lick the paper's edge to stick

oh, the bliss— to watch the sugar
melt from cube to nothingness
in the black of morning coffee
bottom dregs pull at the sips

dark swirling into white
as light caramel shades my cup
you steal a nip, before i sit
your's still too hot to touch

i tangle in your tresses
'fore it's time that we get up
with eyes so brightly open
mouths to kiss so gently shut

grab one more drag of cigarette,
i don't want this to end
maybe we can call in sick
stay home, in love, in bed

| comatose|

sleepless in a shared room
in the detox end of the ward
our beds were split, with a thin blue curtain
mostly to mask my piss breaks
and paper-robe changes

i heard you wheezing, your chest –
breaking to the beat of your heart monitor
as your blood pressure dropped and spiked

and there, was she
she came to you thrice daily
to hold your shoulders
to touch your face and kiss your hands in curl

and before the lights went out
she had already been ripped, halfway down the page
and she'd leave as c o n f e t t i
dropped into the waste-bin of your weathering

you didn't know that she'd come
everyday
and cry on your chest
maybe you heard the soft promises
maybe you felt her nails digging into your wrist
maybe you know
i hope you do

i like to think you said it back to her—

from behind the paper-thin privacy,
 of the half-split blue curtain

| reading glasses |

the time has come
for reading glasses
in the kitchen
for the intricate print
of passed down cookbooks

as their ghosts
move through
my ladles and spoons

the presence
of every former table maker
traditions of the love creators

in every flick of my whisk
every turn of the chicken
in every squeeze of the citrus

and i fondly welcome the company
as i eat until the plate is clean
for i am also growing old myself
now a ghost of my own recipe

of forfeited birthdays
and prescriptions

now arthritic

and completely unable
to
    h
      o
        l
          d

        the weight of my own words
upon the next line

| bone frost |

on organic canvas
the presence of color on frost
stormed in snow
the streets split

like the pages i turn with wet thumbs
and blurred
in the damp of dense weather

it breaks
in winters bone
my mind and spine
a love unborn

as it billows out
my breath before
to watch it go,
to truly know

what cold can be
and do to me

and i am

| antithesis |

i don't say goodbye right
i *irish* the fuck out of it

propagation;
as a limb, the hold it has on the sun
the reach
a gasp in veins waving
when hello meets it's match

i don't say goodbye right
i *irish* the fuck out of it

| where is that mouth full of air |

the quelling quiet
at the end of a voice mail
the ringing that sits beneath the replay
an ocean roar
in the conch framed curve of my ear

my thoughts are
water— a flowing tide

it's only my blood pumping in the echo
it's only the sound of my body,
making itself an island

an ocean roar
if i ever find myself to be,
an island again
surround me in your violent breath

| weigh station |

my toothpick pokes and points
towards road trip diner exits
my gums prodded in fresh stab
i bleed, realizing
my young has been undone

the way it felt to be lost,
in apple pie and gasoline-soaked-blue-jeans
i am a thief of feeling me
it's gone
lost in a brown bag behind truck stops
in payphone sick calls

stabbing my numbed gums and tongue
breathing *midwest* dust for *terra cotta* lungs

i am exhausted
chewing my splintered toothpick
pretending to eat the earth
when i just want to turn around
and drink you in

| a semblance of exits |

a palpable musk of chlorine has flooded in—
from the hallway of an indoor hotel pool
passed over the coarsely thin run carpet
and edged it's scent tightly between the lower doorjambs
sharp enough to taste

and i was getting sick in the bathroom
as you sat on the floor from the other side of the door
head tilted back, talking to the ceiling
pretending that this wasn't the end to our story

i had stayed the night, one too many times
in drunken slumber
and it was leaving me again
the *pbr* purged
from the depths of my over indulgent paunch
i'd muscle out a weak and breathless,
" never agaaiiiin"

and i was leaving you

i was leaving you again,
from a hotel off the highway
our love had finally run its course
and i was leaving you for good

a trembling hand forced
and the day was already half over,
before we were
and we'd leave at separate times
never to speak again
and i got back to all that drinking
'til nary a drop was left in sight

| best out of three |

stashing first aid kits
'cause hurt people, hurt people
rock, paper, scissors

| micro expressions |

we are unhinged
at the crest of our creased kissing lips

with our bones showing through
like the ribs of a stuck pig

we are undone
like the wingspan
of a golden flapping finch

and persistent to begin
oh, petrichor
let your wet petals commence

fill my nose
make us a jerk of jaw,
in allergy season wince

as nosegay does,
the uninhibited flower will stretch

from our roots to our petals
and between of our stems

| becoming. |

in a blinding light we seek forth
to carry new colours to the sunset
we breathe out, only for you to breathe in
we observe with our eyelids shut
we forgive names
we start fires to enjoy rain
we are life, and we are sinners
we are passion
we haven't given up on our daydreams

we celebrate physical senses and dimensions
of time and space
we are walking memories
we do not throw our caution to the wind
as caution is irrelevant when you are in control
we are all in control

we are seeds of our own gardens
we are here and now
we are forever a part of all
we are condensed matter,
swimming in an ocean of sound waves

we are potential change
we are all-ready doing it
we are the movement of colour
and depth and sound and height and growth
we are me, we are you
we are simply complex
we are voiced
we are challenge and we are answers

we were never fighting a battle
therefore
we haven't lost

| *gogh* |

limber river,
beetle black 'neath milky break
ebbs in the bosom of nightshade

a glistening glister

over thundered blubbered bloat
float frothed in viridian iris
the orchestral crickets spin the shore

dripping little starry night
a conch cut as ardent ear
a life begins as sacrifice
my will cannot be veered

| necklace beads, apéritif |

flappers flap in gasper glow
emboldened breath of bitters
stirring, spinning, *sazerac*
loosely dressed in glitter

a fine choice-bit of calico
jazzy jangled jitters
drum brush brought the baseline in
our heals began to skitter

clad of haberdashery
newsboy caps atwitter
wallflower flasks and roaring horns
charleston kicking spinners

swelled the songs on gimlet trips
speakeasy heavy hitters
a whiskbroom's goof to move the room
we found our hearts a flitter

| solomon |

it's hard to feel fresh
in a dead town
hard to build nests
in a campground
same as to a flower
for a bloodhound

it's hard to find rest
without enough money to sleep

| meet me in *montauk* |

a mute swan song
to slow our bones
and probe our wander-lusting full
with head-butted heartbeat
a symposium of silent soliloquy

to be, an exhibition in exhumed iris
to be, crystalline violet
to be, patiently vibrant
to be, the love inside every quiet

to mute;
as our bodies sing electric
our love shall now sing,
besotted and stumbled
in all of its brilliant blindness

ennui : | \ än-ʹwē :
a feeling of weariness and dissatisfaction : boredom

this is nothing new,
just a whole lot more of it

ennui : | \ än-ʹwē :
a feeling of weariness and dissatisfaction : boredom

this is nothing new,
just a whole lot more of it

| man, screaming |

a motivational cat poster
with the caption, "hang in there"
he repositions his necktie
double windsor
takes a break at the brick window

scrolls past a sea—
of influencer's regurgitated encouragements
"instavangelists" : selling thoughts and prayers
a little extra for a mention

but everyone knows,
that the *golden gate bridge,* is the only way to heaven
so when they say jump
he'll scream back in sheepish question,
"how high?!"

| i weird myself out |

we're talking about passion here
and there is a fine fishing line;
between baiting a hook and baiting your breath

a fine power line;
between keeping the lights on
and burning your furniture
we are talking about passion,
hear?

| sans romance |

you were *holy writ,* with trigger fingers
a ball of paper, chewed and spit
you were only meant, to read the cover
but broke my spine, just to get in

| *swedish death cleaning* |

for these things, take time—
the walls thickened film, of old laughs
the way the cold paint, felt hard—
pressed against, my bare back

not just for spring : this cleaning
for our caskets will outlast these bedsheets
let us kneel over them : like an altar
as death is akin to sleep

little wishes : smaller prayers

and as you take unto the closet
i shall pry about— each mothy box
these things are not of us, any longer
for these things, take— time.

and leave us to— unburden the youth—
from these decades of musterings
our collections of mildewed memories
out from the rug, and down from the ceiling

and let go —
as we bare witness—

to a litmus test, for minimalists
what doesn't need, will surely leave
and only keep, that of necessity;

" just some flashlights and our love "
and a few small sakes to keep
for these things— take time
as we are : *swedish death cleaning*

| backstroke |

i cannot ask her again
and the horses are fast asleep in the sun
like plastic toys on their side— in running position

i cannot bare what she might say,
if i spoke of *prague* again
my car idles in the driveway

air conditioner— at full blast
as *atlanta* becomes,
the hot wash cloth— in the sauna of august

i cannot ask her to come along
to run with me
as she does not hold— the same anxious celerity

so i say nothing,
i let her sit— under the red umbrella
her sunglasses pressed closely—
into a modern *austenesque* novel,
as she cooks the white out of her toes

so i walk around the grocery store
and stare at the dead fish on ice
with caught eyes
and maybe if i just cool myself down a bit
like them, the fish
we can call this home

and just be those worry free and natant neighbors
swimming through summer—
for the rest of our lives
or at least until the above ground pool—
breaks at the splitting seems of its bowing sides

| i don't clean myself for me |

my face, blanched and cut with rose
a niacin flush, naive as prose
chattered teeth, bequeathing cold
to spite my face, i cut my nose

orange aura with palpable pulp
belly burnt like gizzards gulp
pathos purge and pencils dull
as writhing hearts are swallowed whole

golden guillotine, ring my neck
picking your brain up off my bed
pillow talk with musky breath
salted skin pressed on my chest

your voice carried out between the sheets
as we robbed the river-banks for free
murders flock and black the sea
i do not clean myself for me

| eager eastward wanderlust |

nail-beds in bits
with an itch for my sore sights to stitch
into the patchwork plains of *pennsylvania*
by chance somewhere in *connecticut,*
there are church bells chiming without cracks

i starve to plant my feet,
into the breeze of coastal seas
maybe i can get mouthy in *maryland*
sup on buttered maize with fish sautéed
and sleep it off in *vermont*
on the porch : of a b & b

as still sings : the violin
to string us all together
under rainy clouds and piano dreams

an itch to surround myself in nautical kitsch
like scratching my skin on a bald tire
a road-trip to end my wandering
take me in:
and i will paint your walls with yellow and grey
as this;
the greatest contrast
the clouds have ever made

| high blood pressure |

humming in ultraviolet
blur of beating wings
twelve hundred heart-beats and counting
stopping for a floral drink

little one, hover me
dip your beak in sugar sweet
hummingbird, for what it's worth
your existence is a masterpiece

| sleep and other things |

a half measure— at half rest
as sleep is—
the estranged bastard half-brother of death

and will it be our dreams—
or might our memories,
be the first to go—
and will our eyes be open—
or halfway closed

| room temperature |

will it be cold?
will it be cold when my relevance whimpers dim
in the dark apartment, with a glass of gin
with the cat clawed couch, and a double chin
will it be cold— when i am no longer him?—
just a shell of skin

will it be cold, on your old side of the bed
when my mind is gone, will the cats be fed?
when my knees give out, and my hair is thin
will it be cold as your hands, caught deathly sick?
when the heat turns off, will it all have been—

worth it?

my decision— to not have kids
my appetite, now crippling thin
will it be cold like the noun or more like the sin
my bulwark walls, built up to brim
so focused on defense, will i forget to live?

will it be cold when i am gone?

it is warm here now— as i am with you
but i fear very soon,
i'll be drinking for two
will it be cold?

| low fuel light [weigh station pt. two] |

i would—
if the road will have me
keep maps folded,
pressed tightly to my chest—
a little to the left

memorizing them—
all by heart : each path
and drive
these are private moments : of silence
stellate and sacred as the night sky opens

i would, if the road will have me
keep going
keep pushing on—
further out, and into the unknown

as if my entire licensed life—
i have been driving
just looking— for the right way
for the right highway to get back home

and i would,
if the road will have me

| crisp |

when will that garden grow?
and how small are we
as shovel and rake

as seed
a watermelon sewn
and forsooth the buzz of birth
shall make them paint the walls new colors
lest they chip
lest the ungloved grip, blister before
the small of our soft splintered skin

such a thing comes with age
callousing with cause
and how small are we
in the end
with sweet-water to sip
with sugared fingers for dirt to stick

in the heavenly height of the sun
and the deepness shared on the ends of our tongues

| tastebuds |

baiting my breath into buttered winds
as high noon swoon in overcast
this is when the crackling clouds begin
rolling smooth— over my sunburnt skin
the old oaks lean their limbs,
into greener keys on blue notes

it is lunch time
so i lay in the front yard and eat with my hands
frisking the feeling of free, in kinetic energy
watching the squirrels flirt—
and taunt the domestic side of the serene

my ears close to the ground
for the telling fruit
of the grandfathered white dandelion whispers
and tickles my whiskers
i need to shave—

and my back is damp with dew
as my face catches drops like i catch connections
this is my favorite part of the day
before the sun is summoned once more
and the wet again turns to burns

so i tread in buttercups, and kelly-green tufts of grassy fronts
to let the flowers flood the taste of my mouth
and the darkened clouds pluck at the love in my lungs
to breathe, in the beauty
that is—
a living daydream

| tracers |

an inch apart, our lips twitch to touch
i pulled traces of light from your eyes—
like heart-strings
—things that were spun from love
as i'd run and sew them into my seams
the nascent to my newly, re-paired dreams

something— the quiet cannot hush

in |earth-play|
the earth quaked
the slightest choke of cherish
to be pitched
sans glint
just after i'd closed my eyes
under florescent flicker
a memoir of gloaming tones

and now to hold—
the most wonderful light
a person— could ever know

| fitting room |

sing now, the puzzle in persiflage pieces
sweet banter in black and white
and tomorrow,
another saw-tooth slice, fits right in
and overmorrow, again

sunday, in chairs that squeak into their rusted frames
to fumble cardboard clouds into a pareidolia prize
nestled and snapped together on the folding table
which is usually used for ironing— the one good shirt i own

we soak, and stare
and piece the curves to square
laughing in frustration
of this pointillism in reverse
and have cigarettes
piece by piece
an outline is nearly there
and stare,
until we can't see straight
and we fold like the table

"okay, tomorrow we will finish it, i just know it"

so we leave the room
and we say goodnight
and kiss quietly with closed mouths

i will see you tomorrow afternoon
and overmorrow
and sundays

| 11:55 |

i am thirty one
i am thirty one and still can't grow a proper beard
i have three chest hairs and i am watching the clock—
count down to midnight
i do this every night
i do this to ensure that i miss the liquor store—
before closing
what a glorious routine
every night
every night i stay up til' three or four
thinking about how i let the liquor store close
thinking how easily i could sleep—
had i not watched the clock count down
i sit and listen to sad songs that make me happy
i read and write and then stare at my computer—
for the rest of the night
i am surrounded by beautiful things,
but all i can see is the clock
its almost here again
another battle with sleep
another war won with the liquor store
and now it is time to stare at my computer screen
i am thirty one
i am thirty one and i am barely sure who i am
i am thirty one
it is now twelve o'won
i am thirty won

| fever dreams |

apricity : the warmth of the sun in winter

i live as *icarus*
melting my wings for a chance to feel it

| memory lain |

atonement : i have scratched my skull full
in the hour of the last letter
the last chance for better weather
the last *danse macabre*— for sad sobs

the last—
blackberry stare into your beautiful pupils
a universe of trueness : and i am become fruitless

as i the naïf—
have trickled into riddles
a puddle of puzzle pieces, that don't have a middle
a thesis of keepsakes, as fevers break brittle

and my language, leaves me languid
lethargic in my limbs, to lift my pen
the last love letter : the last good measure
the last : what could of been

| mt. hood |

and i let go—
so when the blood dries from my nose
you will only know it by the snow
eleven inches— and still storming

if warmth were a color
it would match the stains upon my clothes
and when the blood dries from my nose
you will only know it by my notes

and i let go

| the ocean is on fire again |

she wanted a baby
i wanted an island
the oil and water
unties in the jar

the ocean's on fire again
the rent is past due
and there are no mothers
in *lord of flies*

| death drive |

august aroint;
of your fictive kismet wishes
begone; of your hold
on tiny locked drawers

bestowing below
of their secret love notes
every envelope sealed
with the stammer of my scratchy throat

and i will yell,
howl, wail, bellow, squall, caterwaul
for the unsung lungs
and stomaches that sunk

for every time i was unbrave
for the "right time" moments,
that came and escaped
left quiet enough,
to hear my arm-hairs raise
as the pattern of a shadow,
only weaves of our past ways

this is déjà vu : a screen memory
après nous le déluge
after us, the flood

august unravel!
a backwards blossom into autumn
and take heed : in the next
the breath of driving death
take heed of its speed
and *eros* may be : released
from the *death drive*

...

august begone; of your pining
of your heated heart and of your bleed
august aroint : and un-join : as so have we
let the falling bring flight, of the dying leaves

for a new day will come,
under autumn's auburn sun
and a renewal of rose
and teeth it shall bring

| bookwormfood |

my dreams are;
strings of seedy motel rooms
tucked behind dirt-napping eyes
grown now, very far from the light

a bookworm
becoming worm food
that long-distance-running nap
from a coffin in a cave
a burial of black

the first and last thing i see
before i let that soil stack
and this is every time i die
and then eventually
when i come back

| clinical trial |

i am not a home
a meta form
wearing my age like a rat race
my rising routine
of coffee and nicotine
followed by a lull—

a steady low
of serotonin
and self sabotage

i must learn to leave time restraints for the rodents
need be—
to stop pandering to the sales schemes
of someone else's dream

what new car smell of fresh hell
as the pleasantries of modernity disquiets me
and do not bury me : in dead dirt
for i have seen the sharp dark

as now, we are merely defined—
by what we leave behind

and i don't want to be what you do

| orangethorpe |

a sunset lawn chair
the breeze blocks are working well
the night is lukewarm

a sunset lawn chair
the breeze blocks are working well
the night is lukewarm

| playing posthumous |

melancholia finds—
such puddled place
as a leak
the flower pot, the faucet,
the old ceiling beams

though it is kind enough,
to leave me be— in sleep
tiptoeing on the hardwood in the hallway

i am lucid, wedged—
between a doublespeak
like the way every welcome mat—
on the way out reads
" olləy / goodbye",
it was just a dream

a weathervane, a window,
a knot of bed sheets
my spine curled into—
a full fetal physique
in a sweat that remains—
to be unbroken for weeks

melancholia finds—
such puddled place
as a leak

what dreams may come
a bed,
and what is underneath

| heroine den |

a swamp of clothing on the floor
a three-ring-circus-tent fell;
center folded
pinpricked into the bounty of our pull out couch

we made out
like bandits
we passed out
like tired rabbits

i wished i was not so pragmatic
i woke into smoke
billowing out from our habits

a dark shower in the sink
cupping my hands underneath—
the soft water to drink

— my thoughts sobered—

for the sum of a few seconds
i found a momentary purpose
in the adrenaline of cleanliness

still shaking
i scavenged through the couch's cracks
and the pockets of my pants
i found a few coins, a crumpled wrapper, a double shot of
vodka, and a pen

finally— i found a lighter
and then i found you again

| one night stand |

the city, sleeps in
illuminated boxes
stacked neon coffins

| one night stand |

the city, sleeps in
illuminated boxes
stacked neon coffins

| ursa major / ursa minor |

seismically super-positioned spoons
d i p p e d & l a d l e d
the naked night, of two spines
c u r l e d & c r a d l e d

an evolution in fusion
call us cutlery : call us beasts
with two backs : butterflied
call us ursa : a bear : a northern light

connecting the dots into lines in the sky
all teeth : all soul : just you and i
call us polaris, and call us constant
call us whatever you'd like

call us intrepid : or call us space-dust
call us beautiful, and call us l o v e
call us e t e r n a l : call us enough
as we begin burning : just call us the sun

endless as infinity
as one plus one equals one

| tether |

the world becomes a very big place,
when the weather begins to warm again

ah yes, the sweet new charm of summer
 like a toothy marmalade,
preserved all winter
to burst across the sky in dripping whimsy
the world becomes a very big place indeed

nostalgia; and all of its nosy magic
resuming my senses back;
into old times, into old lives
into all the little poignant moments of perfection
 the simple serendipities

resting in the heat,
as we'd brave the windows and their possible insects
wide open
for the prospect of the perfect breeze

smally sprawled out on the couch
with fresh white socks and exposed virgin-winter-skin
 sinking our bones into sad songs
with *bright* eyes on even brighter days

the wool, of the cottonwoods
pulled to end, in the red tepid air
the idea of love : or something close
so close we could smell it

resumed

the world becomes a very big place,
when the weather begins to warm again

| fruit stand |

a mewling squeak
of sunken teeth
piercing deep
in fuzzy peach

dribble slow sweet nectar

as summer offers its sugary sweet
we offer ourselves to each other

| touch touché |

on guard!
thief of thunder
trinket trapper
spurring urchin from depths below

for you, succubus!
soul of mold
raven maven
murder mouthed in blackened tone

for i, lonesome lover!
lain the line
conquered conquest
and walls have grown

on guard!
tilted taker
in muted milieu
underwater & overthrown

on guard!

| after midnight |

i'm so tired of feeling like a sequence of orgasms
the only thing i look forward to,
after dividing my finances for the week
here's for rent, for my car, for petrol,
for my phone, and food, electric,
for the heat, a/c, etc.

that five second rush
and then back to the dishes, the laundry,
the tedious weather chats
 my neighbors waving like they know me

i'm so tired of feeling like a machine
like the only reason i function is to fuck or to be fucked,
like the only thing that keeps me running
are these well lubricated parts
and the possibility of procreating another desk job applicant

| was this helpful |

nearing my thirty fifth identity crisis
underwhelmed;
in a dive-bar parking lot
waiting for lightning to strike twice

and if home is where the heart is,
where do my organs exist?
where does my blood live,
when my heart becomes homeless

a sickness : all condolences
something unpronounceably malignant
the doctors will say cirrhosis

and everything is a paid advertisement
preying on our instincts
our emotions,
our humanity, our brokenness, our souls
to refill our cups and our voids and our houses,
our stomachs and their rolls

lonesome and overstimulated
chasing that liquid good time feel,
of a languid liquored lobotomy
friday bleeds into *monday*
like an over-saturated paint tag
when working for the weekend,
used to hold some kind of meaning

| the everglow |

last year's leaves—
dead but not gone
un-mulched; and matted to the mud
pressed dense below skinny spears of grass
the wild land *grows taller : at night*

a tabernacle of turning
the sun-shy of fireflies
come to worship at dusk
the everglow
the wonder of spontaneous combustion
if we were all so lucky
to stay long enough to see the spark

| laughing at cornstalks |

like the final moments of an ice-cube
i have become, melted for you
dripped to dust, in dark wet membrane
in the seared stubborn sizzled stretch of summer
the dry heat of high noon

these are the dog days

and might my love then offer me grace
to wait—
for my return as rain
as i— a chapfallen flounder
in this golden sea of maize
to wait—

for the touch of your love
and warmth of your rays

to bring every ice and every ache,
of my humbled heart : to melt away
to heat within your light
to drip to dust and evaporate

| young louvre |

the sound of our spent knuckles
an attaching sort of crackling
the art of you to open up
from heart-crafted paper gift-wrapping

we are pliable as putty
twisted up together, like twine
in mirth of many endless blessings
the first time we shared the night

| saccharine dreams |

i click on the stove
as the back burner glows
a fiery branding-iron red
the kettle calls for the cup
hisses and whistles

like a sentient machine,
courting the tea
as tonight it seems,
ashwagadha it will be

i pour the steam
and steep the leaves
milk or cream
honey sweet

fleetly read some poetry
brush my teeth
and deeply breathe

count some sheep beneath the sheets
rest my head, and go to sleep
nightly wish for it to be
forevermore, the sweetest dreams

| the poet's prayer |

our author, whom art in hologram
followed be thy name
thy rhythm come, thy likes be thumbed
in books as it is online
give us this day, our daily prompts
and forgive us our hash-tagging
as we forgive the algorithms against us
and lead us not into stagnation
but deliver us from dribble
for thine is the rhythm, the power and the story
forever and ever,
refresh

| healthcare is hard to come by |

i sold the car, that we used to have sex in
   this morning, i ate some cheesecake for breakfast
i guess what i am trying to say is— that—
all things that feel good; are
until it's time for goodbyes and the bill

| chromatophores : *pigment-bearing cells that cater for the ability to shift body coloration and pattern to provide dynamic camouflage* |

the shape of naked
i stare : examine my cells
my unforgiving liver
my sporadic heart murmurs

i posture my pear-like shadow
into an akimbo peter pan stance,
dancing in limbo
a pitcher of milk with two handles

something about sleeping alone
and shedding,
like a corn husk, or stardust
with a glistening missing

staring: watching my color change
the pattern of age;
is camouflage : lest any of us talk
of death or love : or at all

just moss : stoic rock : stubborn
lest we make room
for something bigger
something more than just killing time
something beyond the greater space,
for a growing gut to find

| patience is suffering with grace |

a mirror and a maze
one gets out alive
glass takes one million years to disintegrate
how rich do you feel?

| pulpit free + calcium |

she walks with god in her pocket
i walk agent-less : in lumbering stumble
striding s i d e w a y s
on the right side of the slightly bright,
fine white lines of the night-time highway

h e a d l i g h t s blinding

today marks the day
i am seven years of new cells
five times over
praying i don't become prey
she prays for people
i always pray for me

it is staggering,
how much roadkill there is—
left behind to behold
when the rat race you're running,
one day, starts to grow slow

and out here, in the cross-hairs
of treaded tires and lifted grills
nothing gets a bible reciting
nor a proper b u r i a l

| carryon |

crows running riot
above honey locust trees
behold, death's circle

244

| roll credits |

an arc : a climaxing
a promise made in post-coital proclamation
a choice to be
a choice of which theatre, will screen our movie

and i have climbed the thoughts of your body
captivated
your adjoining soul
and my own bag of bones

the greatest reminders of time
moving on; like a gentle cry
to know that it is you,
that i desire
to love until i die

so onwards, sideways and outcries
as the moral of a good ghost story
is to always try and stay alive

| church coffee |

crumpled notes
of favorite poems
what damning thought
it is to know

that this will all be over soon

before our children grow old enough to make mistakes

| heavy metal hardware |

the tumbling stones in your gut
the crunch and stir of bolts and nuts
and secrets
loosely unthreading
your promise to keep them

it is vinegar and vile and calculated
and so you scream acidic
in abstract cacophony
with machines you scream

and scream
you squeal and shriek and sing
until you are red
and then you are blue

and now you are mauve

| machinery |

no windows at work
midnight oil, burns fluorescent
night is day is night

no windows at work
midnight oil, burns fluorescent
night is day is night

| i've slept better in hospitals |

it's the gravel betwixt my eyes and lids
the whites are bright and carmine
blood banked, so drained
so dry from staring at the future

i can't even see my own two feet in front of me
scavenging for sparks
like a carrion crook, devouring dazzle
to fill, the dead parts of myself

hovering the desert for a hologram of hindsight
and these canines
are looking to sharpen
on some special kind of sparkle
but mirage is always the moniker of the *midwest*

with crosses and scorched asphalt
both burn at these altitudes

: so i stay indoors :

where i can sleep
and i can drink
where god can't see me
with just the quiet of my hiding
and another refill on my i.v.

| gypsophila |

to be again
and untouched
as *tabula rasa*
born bathed in warm web
of gentle feathers
of slacked milk-cotton spread

spider-white : the whispered branch
anew ; in bunch the baby's breath
as gossamer span
stretched to swaddle and annexed in

caught leaf that turn to yellow-red
wander autumn to deaden sense
still to carry the comfort summer
tabula rasa : to be again

| hemosiderin |

somethings, don't wash out
like words when you mean them

i try soft landings, but coughs happen
unable to separate my heart from my thoughts
my thoughts from my words
my words from my mouth
my mouth from your ears

the cutting abruptness of, " i *love you*"
now spoken out loud

and then; a galaxy sized silence
followed by your rigid reply of indifference
pull it back
pull it back
god, please let me unsay it!

gasping : trying to suck the words right out of the room

my mouth caught it's bitter bite back
like splinters
like stripper glitter
sticking;
unto the dark burgundy upholstery of my cheeks
something that burrowed into my pre-bedtime anxieties
for the next few weeks

maybe she'll forget about it, if i just get myself clean
a bath drawn with *epson salt*
as it filled up to my knees
somethings don't wash out : like permanent ink
as i am too grown for the tub now
and the water is overflowing

| utility bill |

between a bundling of bedding
we were braided to be
rows; of symmetry
under tungsten tainting

starved to tangle, up—
 within the knots of you
massaging your skull,
looking for birthmarks
frazzled
working the nerve,
to leave the apartment

a pashmina flipped
for your exposed skinny neck
when the time comes
to skate or skip
on winters lip
i will always wish
to brush your hair,
next to the accordion of radiator

| dazzle miasma |

soft instrument of impression
a masterpiece composes
in sculpting smoke
cigarettes; as metaphor for silhouette and blink
as aesthetic of angel and scream
painting music from empty
shimmer it's rhythm, on lively leaves

soft instrument of impression
a masterpiece composes
in sculpting smoke
cigarettes; as metaphor for silhouette and blink
as aesthetic of angel and scream
painting music from empty

| wet blanket |

i loosen myself
like a pack of matches
a bonfire probing my thoughts

fanning the fiery waves
of dead pine within my mind
how those aching cinders
and embers would snap

how they would kiss and hiss
in the heart of the heat
like we used to

but now; we just kiss like *sisyphus,*
pushing that rock up
only to roll down
back onto the fire
smothered

oh, that pine
that loosened lit log
that just couldn't quite catch

might a cold be caught far quicker
than the late of our fizzling flame

| nightcrawler |

in the hour of bright wilt
and sun golden spilt milk
dusk shakes the dawn
in parentheses pause
of pitch-black

as return the moonlit silhouette
of the graveyard-shifters
cast and crew of skeleton drifters
in midnight overtime neon

here without sun or shadow
working the floorboards like flowerbeds
the dancers in the dark

the movers and shakers for early-time wakers
the marquee spacers and weather news chasers
unseen as you sleep
between parentheses
of pitch-black

as dusk shakes the dawn
in the blue morning calm
you will start the day off
where they are
and have been
all along

eyelids taped open
i'll be worthless tomorrow
but tonight, is mine

eyelids taped open
i'll be worthless tomorrow
but tonight, is mine

| crash |

something not so different
from a tin can crushed
or loves first rush

we sit
with shards of windshield
embedded into our skin
our lips
our *achilles heels*

laughing in the backseat of the crashing
with broken hearts and bloodied mouths
as no one has ever said,
that stop signs actually work
and we were just kids,
that never learned
how to slow down

| folie à deux|

the warmest summer sparkle
coaxed bashful over maddened minds
sharing beds for ballroom trysts
as wicked whistles harmonize

mutually assured destruction
delivered dourest paradigm
to love you like an arsonist
to burn in fields like parting tides

we follow charred up footprints
to bathe once more in bedroom eyes
my devil darling dangle
my bleeding sleeve, my blinded pride

doomed since the day assembled
to wish for less a kismet time
to play the pandering partner
committed to the perfect crime

folie à deux : we atrophy
our lunacy has multiplied
a severing of you and me
and live alone : or surely die

| the last happy camper |

melting potential
on waning wings of wax
of borrowed time
i am become,
ostracized
like analog
in whimsy of split lip
a lack of laughter
dreams drip
in puddled sun
as i am unwritten
to drown
in my own manifesto
as the last happy camper

| ikigai |

what purpose could i find
in the totems left behind?

these rosaries and roses and flesh
all of which are worshiped
through holy stained glass
all five of my right fingers spread
 and pressed against it

an artist with stigmata
the apertures of my hands expand
what water could wash these wounds
what love could fill their gaps

what purpose is the blood
if wasted in the heart
for ever the oil painting
that i could never seem to start

: or never quite dried :
where does it hide,
my ikigai

what mess i've made to mean something
what purpose is my last name
to be remembered
for at least one or two more decades

as the dust of my paint brush—
steeps to clean in linseed jars
i search again for purpose
in the paint of pain for honest art

| old pipes |

for seventeen years— i've been stewed to the gills
a bent elbow; tipping over bar stools
the underwhelming continues

and it takes a mighty crack
to warrant such a terminal approach
a harrowing heartbreak
the lines start to blur overtime

i lost myself somewhere
staring down that long glass neck
in every pull, and every nip
in the black of losing consciousness

it takes a triumphant fracture
to bring about such a burst
and it's hard to contain a flood
with blood as thin as piss

| paper mill |

umber pines stood staunchest
over crumbed stumps of fallen trunks
paint draped onto a pine-needle easel
in meshed depth of stacked lash

as a malignant moon swoon
to death rattle black
my shoes moved in shuffled muffle
beneath the thick grass

dividing the dark
as coarse the path cracked
with bouldering boots, i scurried on past
with one bum leg and an even worse back

so utterly desperate
to leave these woods fast
or possibly : perhaps
just to finally outrun
my god damned past, at-last

| picker |

be it weather, or not
that stripped car will sit
in a junkyard
rusting out— like our high-mileage hearts
cadaverously still
at the intersection of guts and glory
feast or famine
and might a resourceful hobbyist,
come scavenge its scraps
for the perfect replacement part
or maybe just an up-cycled garden planter

| banana bag |

i am a scribbled gibberish
on a hospital bed in the hallway
i watch as the nurses wheel a new neighbor over
on a gurney with a tourniquet : he is losing his leg
and his eyes were as yellow as two street lamps
in a heavy fog : jaundiced as a tennis ball
i am sure he has seen far too much death for one lifetime

i lay curled and convulsing on a cot
as visceral witness
my neighbor is losing his leg
and i am losing my god damn mind
they come with a cart to check my vitals
heart racing like a rabid rabbit
and i may have seen far too much death for one lifetime

they stitch me intravenously with a *banana bag*
attempting to sew me up : of every gash and prod
from every devil and drink
that's burrowed their way into my belly
and i lay on my back, stiff as a board and shaking,
as a draft slipped up my gown

i think of rings : one of the wedding variety,
wondering; if my hands would ever bare their metal
semblance : or if i even wanted them to

two : i think of a cigarette, spilling smoke rings,
circling out from my cheeks; god i would kill for a
cigarette right now

lastly; i think of my gripped ring around the neck of
a bottle. the neck of every single bottle i'd swallowed to
get myself here in the first place
wondering; exactly which ring would finally be the
untimely death of me
        it's the latter i suppose

| the stall of vitriol |

calligraphic cat-calls
subtle kitschiness of claw
an affinity for alchemy
mysterious & flawed

broken hooves on *clydesdales*
culled biggest hearts to maul
decadent in scripture
when *rome* began to fall

candescent is the glowworm
silk spinning cavern walls
echoing in plainsong
a caveat to all

calligraphic cat-calls
innocently scrawled
baroque as bloodied inkwells
my book on how to stall

| wharffle cone |

at the liminal base
where the overlap fades
as the last few grains
of bleached sand breaks
and the wooden walk
of boat-docks sway

there is a felicity

ninety something degrees
with the dog on a leash
get him water to drink
in the shade of palm trees
we move to the stand
for a treat by the sea

there is a simplicity

for our hot summer tongues
mouths moving to meet
to thaw down the scoops
mountain mounds of ice cream
no cares of the drip
nor that of the stick
a cup or a cone
"so what'll it be?"

to let the inner child speak

| chroma |

i, in strongest *millefleur*
pose my strongest poesy
as we all fall down
ring round the subtle sound
of growth in silent slumber

and not to rot
or dry
or die
we are the earth
and we are birth

we are
perennial in posture
as sleeping winter, wakes
and again
the seeds do grow

| blood bugs |

there has been a hijacking
a heist, of my blood
the mosquitoes digesting
fresh drops in their gut

back yard's now a crime scene
legs itch from the bumps
leeched lips are still smacking
six needles in one

my veins, they are mining
the levee to flood
i swat where they're dining
but more seem to come

in sweat they will find me
from water they've sprung
vampires of the bug world
to burgle my blood

| ultraquiet |

april fools is behind us
and i have sat in many rooms,
with many tables, in many homes

unable to lift my lips, from the upright and locked position
 and not a grace nor graze has passed their pucker
in seven long months— mostly the cold ones

and i still taste you when it's raining

still wonder how you're doing
hoping your table is full
of light and good friends,
and their dogs,
that scurry 'round the dinning room chairs
turning the hardwood into a skate-rink

and maybe if we sit still enough,
we can still hear the weathervane on the rooftop,
creaking in the wind

if we listen hard enough,
we can still hear,
the last breath that escaped the gap from our mouths—
when we slowly pulled away

| parachute |

the thing about f a l l i n g : in love
is that the other person is supposed to catch you—
way before you hit the ground
and yet, sometimes—
all that is left,
is a splattered imprint
of what your insides used to look like

| brumal |

watch this countryside closely
as it rests
golden, brittle and birdless
in the window of winter
staging itself to sit stiffly in silent burden

as we all have
at the bottommost closing of our crops
after the harrow of annual harvest
the revenant ritual of rotation

with white exhaust clouds, billowing from my mouth
i follow the map of sallow fields
standing low and firm in hibernation

feeble rows, now digesting their own necks
and just beneath the earth,
the ashen echoes of soil—
rigidly grip the tender ends of their headless roots

a frosty afterthought of frozen gale—
sweeps in deeply from the east
to season the rounded metal slants—
of silo rooftops with shiny stellate frosted fingerprints

watch this countryside closely
for if you aren't looking
with eyes undivided
in the overzealous hour of sundown
the interstate will be quick to leave you
standing cold and sightless in the dark
as it slowly pulls back at the light from the city
the sun
and every stolen star

| present company included |

let's get sad together
that kind of painful pleasure
strung out on earl grey and elliott smith
misery loves a good company party

| plenty of ish |

my soft spots
what do they look like?
the released chink—
in the scales of my sea-stripped armor

white underbelly
a gut, nonetheless
a bucket
for corn cobs and clam shells
empty me

wet napkins
with chicken-scribbled phone numbers
three sheets smeared
into their disintegrating layers
butter and *cajun* seasoning

my soft spots : your *soup du jour*
with spoon to scald
a chowder mouth
unfastened
to cook the last singular cell—
of it's pinkish soft palate

| the collector |

superfluous in feel
every sense of spirit
collecting bones and marrow
muscles and organs

from the chest of men
recidivism sits on my shoulder
chewing and spitting
a linger i negotiate to trade

i beg and barter
to not latch on
that teat
of anguished inevitability

i am a vessel of headstones
electrocardiogram, without pulse
i am a body bag
every sense of spirit

making distance of vision
evaporating
like the spilt milk
which we were never supposed to cry over

| walk in the park |

whoa, the atrophy!
the retrograde
the splint stiffened over—
my fragile snapped leg

and every time i try—
 to walk a new path
i find a better concrete
a harder curb to collapse

buildings;
are just places—
that people try not to die in

| juice bar |

gravity asks far too much of us
of our heaviness
the anvils of past baggage
weighing down in full tilt

and we carry it's bulk
deeply within our viscera
it is tightly sewn into our sinew,
into our bones

its gristle : something indigestible
so just : keep : on : c h e w i n g

but could it be?
that through this carnage,
in the tenderness of our tendons
and relentlessly gripped fists

that the effort of juice,
which drips between our fingers
might just be worth it,
enough to endure
that ever seemed
asphyxiating squeeze...

| pressure cooker |

nine fourty-three p.m.
there she is again
in the corner of the living room
lounging under the quilt that her best friend made her for
christmas
feet up : on her grandmother's old off-green ottoman
watching tv, while simultaneously scrolling her phone
and kneading the cats paunch
just waiting : with fat eyes
to see if i go to the garage again
to see if i'll get another drink

just waiting to say something
her jaw set like a pressure cooker
i wish she would just go to bed already
i'm not drunk enough yet
and i really don't want another argument tonight

so i make up a lie
say i have to go get more cigarettes
ask her if she wants anything
she always says no

but i know that she wants something
she wants to say something again about my drinking
i sigh, "okay then, be back soon"

and even though i'm barely buzzed now
i take the back-roads to the gas station
quickly grab my stash and belly up to the counter
for a six pack of tallboys,
some jerky and a pack of wintergreen gum

...

take the same back-roads home,
pull in and park with the lights off
steadily slam four beers in the driveway
and cram the other two in my coat

i try to walk in casually
which really didn't matter
as she was already in bed by the time i got back
with every light cut off and every door bolt locked

i could see the glow from her phone in the bedroom
as she signed off and set it on the charger
turned over solemnly,
with a quick rustling of sheets and a small mousy cough

the house was dead, pin-drop silent,
so quiet
that i could hear my blood rushing through my ears

i snuck out to smoke one more cigarette
 and slam the other two beers
stumble in and pass out on the couch
with the t.v. on

eleven thirty-two p.m.
and here i am again
in the corner of the living room
ending another night, cheating on her
with my one and only, my first love, my first buzz

and she will eventually leave me one day
as she surely and rightfully should
but if i am to be completely honest,
i'd rather be drinking here alone,
in peace
with the cat, who's got nothing to say

| carpenter in the apiary |

a cluster of carpenter bees hover outside the entrance of my
apartment building's stairwell
like floating gargoyles
guarding the summer castle
suspended
and zipping their rotund yellow-furred bodies about
with tiny little wings

they don't bother me much though
as i am not a flower
nor am i a tree, or a piece of wood siding
to be chiseled into with their sturdy micro-mandibles

male carpenter bees don't have stingers,
so they just fluff their fur and try to act tough
however, the female bees can sting like a son of a bitch
they don't bother me much though
as long as i leave them be

see, everything has a threshold
a limit to enduring external aggravations
even the sweetest bee in the apiary
can bite back, if you provoke them enough
humans are the same

so i maneuver past the buzzing flutter and into the cool of
the air conditioned building
most good things have a threshold
i try to remember these things
when admiring the beauty of the natural world
and all her pretty little sharp objects

| quilt |

its the rusted metal fan-blades,
that skin the muggy air of its slimy surface
a blade of grass between my thumbs
a duck call

the tinsel-thin blade that bows,
on the choppy shadows of my jaw line
the watery blood drop that rivers my neck
from its sharpened stainless edge

a blade against the ice,
shaving snow-cones at the heal of your skate
the switchblade that you carry at night
the same one that you hate

all of these tools
these blades
and if they could speak
might they tell me how to cut away,

how to chop at the breadth, of the time and space—
that has grown within the cracks of our absence
the vastly compromised terrain

a place, that we no longer even exist in
to scissor through the thicket of division
to find the missing
and sew the memory of our intimacies
back in to our tattered stitchings

| a bar of departure |

a scattered passenger,
with small prose of hope
a gadabout garnished,
with nihilistic undertones

solitary sets in,
and i don't answer the phone
now i'm tipsy-tilted-gripped
and i am swerving back home

a calamitous custom,
i would hardly condone
as i try to get clean,
yeah, as dry as a bone

but the bar fly's are buzzing
and won't leave me alone
we are swallowing our problems
without somewhere to go

only later we'll reap
all the shit we had sewn
and tonight i've decided
i will leave on my own

quite heavily bent
and as pale as a ghost
as i shut my left eye
and turn down the radio

god, i promise i'm done
if i make it back home
as i pray to the sky
that i don't miss the road

| davenport |

my madness has been dredged from blot
a *rorschach* inked, my milk-spilt rot
and cars sing loud, put up on blocks
and drugs and birds and morning coughs

i want to love, a lofty lot
the way they tied, forever knots
my grandpa shakes, his heart was lost
as grandma's urn now gathers dust

| canteen |

at the water again, without plan
my mouth : a dried up wishing well
and this is not a desirable scene to drink
the brown cackling of wetland
babbles on
meanwhile—
my throat salts in the shadeless sun
the untouched mud— rubbers
underneath my feet
and surely, the only thing that would live here
is something far more dangerous,
than i would care to swim with

| the drip |

there is something about a waxed wing
that water doesn't waste

there is something about a waxed wing
that water doesn't waste

| afternoon simulation |

in the sky made of cell phone signals
a dark blue balloon : drifts along

in the contrails—
of a big black breathtaking bird
as they both soar to scrape their shadows
against the surface of the slender clouded ceiling

i cut my losses
like a loose thread
and allow my hopes to float
right on up : past both

the synchronicity,
is astonishing
i am astonished : i am a bird
i am bursting in the thinning air : a bubble

like a dark blue balloon : popping
with its string cut
and no one around tall enough,
to jump up and grab it

| two minus one equals zero |

from what widower's window
would the glass be different
a tinge of ruby,
meets the bottom of the mountain's kneel
gone now—
are the frogs, perched on tree limbs
no longer to pearl the rained-out flies,
on the round of their overdrawn pouts
gone is their bark—

and lost is our sight
as our heavy eyes retire
now sunken beneath the night
closed up like the windows
and air tight as an alibi

when will that window change its scenery
and could i decide to open it
if you will never be here to see

| as above |

this mid-morning is;
quite mundane
and drenched
in the cool-wet-empty of *january*

the horizon,
a water colour of dampened echoes
as it's steady drizzle;
h o l d s   m e
under the half-roof awning of the balcony

my lips pursed
around the rim of my wide-mouth mug
my favorite eggshell-white coffee cup
catching the grounds

the last bitter leftover bits
of *french-pressed* dregs

a s   i   s p i t

with my teeth to tongue
and a cloud for breath
there is green behind my neighbor's white picket fence

and as above
s o   i t   i s   b e l o w

the rain and the sound of heaven crashing
birds in the belfry, fog on the ground

i wish you were here

| duster/sifter |

" you don't know the half of it "
i shuttered
as if i could quantify my dejection
with basic butchered baking measurements

a metric peg in an imperial hole
a gram of the good stuff
sixteen hundred kilometers away
you don't know the half of it

a reference to cups of sugar
eight tablespoons to go
before that cup overflows
or four ounces if that is faster

| locksmith |

belt loop, hip cliffhanger
dangle the overstuffed split-ring
the carabiner
i hold on to— too many keys for one being
implied walls, for exhausted locks
the moment you approach
my fox-holed heart
first met, by an armory of arteries
and no one gets in alive

| forest code |

a feral black cat
or more so, a mangy grey—
if a certain sun catches
begins a trot : an off-broadway ballet
swift to strut
across the leafy breach of the dark green tree-line

mouth wet and painted bright red
from the feathers and blood like brake fluid—
of a small windless cardinal
eyes forward and dead set
onto the next—
of dinner destination

but now with heavy head—
ungracefully tilted
weighing top-down and strongly to the left
sore and unbalanced and scratching—
at the mites and the ticks

as a congregation has gathered
of rebellious pedestrians
that now rent the king's ear
as a passing party tent

| trash night |

if i had your grip,
could i then properly pulverize this?
this germless gem inside my chest
if i had your grip—

could i then compress it?
this fossilized knot of driftwood;
to black powdery ash
could i crush this pyrite cluster;
positioned left beneath my breast
could i then squeeze it—

possibly hard enough to prove honey?
or rain water : could i?

that fleeting feeling ferments
an oozing booze— to let
could i then throw it on the fire
for one more warm night to spend
just one more night, like when we first met

before your palms close in, to tightly grip—
around the top of a tall kitchen trash bag
before you take my rotten radish of a resting heart rate—
out—
    for a final nettled acquainting—
with the bottom leftovers of the *tuesday* night bin

| long distance runner |

boyington and *duffie* oaks sway
the way i tend to lose balance, in all the wrong ways
i sat and smoked my windows yellow
watching the vines take hold of the interstate

treading the dis-connectivity—
atop the loose gravel ground
rolling my ankles running,
for a cause i know nothing about

run
all i do is run

though everything is close, and pretty and perfect—
with side-blinders
"you must run!"
my only inner dialogue
you better run
while you still can...

run
until you can't feel the rapacious and relentless wrench
the wretched weight
of everything
of anything you had ever once meant to own

< < < r u n > > >

| smoking will kill you |

there is a moth in the bucket
the old lidless dry-wall-putty container,
that sits under the flood light on the side of the house
it catches dead leaves,
rain water, and hot tobacco cherries that i flick out from my
half smoked cigarettes
it's been filling for a month
and is more like watery-tar at this point

and now, there is a moth in it
it's five thirty a.m. and i am just about to leave for work
i smoke half a cigarette before i get in my car
and a moth is in drowning in the tar bucket
i stand there for a few drags
and watch as the moth flops around,
 flapping it's stressed out wings; it's too early to think
but i am posed with a matchstick-sized moral dilemma

do i stand here and do nothing; do i just watch the moth die?
do i let nature take its course?
i mean, why should i care?
moths don't show any sign of perceived sentience
they wouldn't respond to a name
hell, they wouldn't even remember me saving it
but before i could contemplate all of the potential moral
choices to make in this butterfly effected brainteaser

that little matchstick sparked a tiny fire inside my gut
it only took about twenty seconds to decide,
if i was an apathetic *darwinist* or a god-playing empath
i chose the latter, and plucked that little bastard out by its
chalky wet wing

...

it fluttered about on the dirt, like a dog shaking off mud
and slowly gained the ability to fly again
moving right on up, through the cigarette smoke and
crashing— right into the flood light

*ping *plink *bzzz : moths are really dumb
that moth will probably be dead in the tar-water thirty
minutes after i leave

but i was able to start my day off—
feeling like a little less of an asshole
so i guess i got that going for me

i stepped on a centipede later that night

| pinkies up |

in the nexus of nesting
we happen : as learned doves
or perhaps;
just some sort of striven likeness
callow in wet membrane

as mothers make tea out of their daughters
little cups, stained
with the inherited tears of oolong
fathers build walls out of their sons
brutish bloodletters
fish out of water
the first of fire
and prized in hunt—

of porcelain
a level does not become
never taught, to sip softly
and oh, what dread might come
might dust behind those blue-glass doors of the china cabinet

| paper trail |

medical bills pile
the good times are killing me
the bad times are too

| paper trail |

medical bills pile
the good times are killing me
the bad times are too

| preserves |

low hangs the heavy fruit
as the impotent limbs frown in their weight
a sweeter sadness still
and i pick them with hands of *eden*

we are sad, because we ate
we are sad, because we are

such a decadent pear to behold
sadness is fruit : sadness is truth
the greatest despondency to chew
yet i still desperately salivate,
to drown in those mighty marmalades

| e |

within the discipline of your lips
there is an urgency
a whiplash : a mewl

a gravity that breaks my body

a tasting : a tickle : a fever
i am tongueless to touch their temper
and storied in the aftermath

a song sharpens on their half closing
and i still hear it; in abandoned places
i still sing it in my sleep : and in the car—
and then the crashing

as when that first kiss—
  had taken all of the weight from my mouth
from the apex of any a heaven's height
i was no longer afraid to fall

| 1.618 |

the axis of morrow
spins a supple and unrestricted self
a taffy; pulling tombs like pottery clay
around this continuum of *untils*

our backs are, the slowest scar
supine in conveyor-belt stargaze
subtle to scrape, above fissured earth
young plates pushed up, to break old skin

navel moon, ghost of morning glory
draws back, as cerulean sheers hang
a bathwater returned to the cyclical sea
as the axis of morrow, spins our drains

A B O U T   T H E   A U T H O R

joshua tool was born in the late evening of *black friday,* in a border town of south *tex-as.* soon to move, a little under a year later to *new york* with military father *john* and mother *trudy.* it is most likely, that this type of sporadic military travel and many more to come in childhood, would be the underlying spark for his undying wanderlust.

at age four, soon after his brother *derek* was born, it was then off to a new destination in the *midwestern* hills of *south dakota.* a dramatic change from the upstates of the north east. he then proceeded to enter school one year early, the first time observation and adaptation made itself to be a new and necessary skill. making and changing his way through public schools while both parents worked full time in addition to second jobs. his first passion was music. either dad was drumming on the table to classic rock ballads or mom was enjoying the dancier side of disco. music was everything to *josh,* a friend that he could take anywhere with him. of all things about music that he enjoyed the most. it was reading the lyrics. he would spend countless hours listening to favorite artists and reading along to their mesmerizing lyrics. this grew into the passion and hope of one day becoming a front-man and writing his own lyrics. until then, he carried on, absorbing all of the magic that music had to offer and inspiration to create by it.

at age twelve it was off to the snow capped peaks of *colorado,* to finish out the rest of school and part of young adulthood. though at age fourteen, depression hit him for the first time. nearly crippling him in bed for a month. without a band yet, he found his outlet in poetry. filling books and books of his dreams and fears and every little thing in between.

this carried on for most of high school, but would fall to the back burner when at seventeen he started his first band! being a very eclectic music enthusiast himself, it only made sense that the bands to follow after the first one would jump around genres dramatically, from death metal to acoustic love songs to avant-garde hip hop tracks, there was never something he didn't want to try. at twenty-one, *joshua* moved to *hollywood california* to get some change and maybe a big break!

joining as lead vox in another *los angeles* metal band, it was something that was soon to fizzle out within his musical and artistic daydreams. as *hollywood was quick to grow exhausting and* old, it was back to *colorado* for a few years before the itch to travel hit again. placing him in the *pacific northwest.* specifically in *central washington state,* where he and a few other friends would start up a *spoken word* group. and very unforseen, it had taken off like a western wildfire! moving from five friends in a living room, to standing only night clubs. this group carried on for a few years and then eventually faded out. still stuck with the taste of spoken word in his mouth, *joshua* was desperate to keep it going. but the party people were separating from the alcoholics, and he was steadily showing signs of the latter. through years and years to follow he would be in and out of hospitals and rehabs, struggling through serious addiction and depression, just as he felt at fourteen. and so, he got back into the simple art of written poetry. this continued to grow and polish as he made another move to *colorado* where he published his first two collections "love nest death bed" and "cryptic flowers", then it was a jaunt to *south carolina, georgia* and now currently of twenty-twenty-one he is back in *california.* over three years after his second collection "cryptic flowers" had been released, the third and full length collection is here. *sleep and other things shaped like death.*

www.ingramcontent.com/pod-product-compliance
Lightning Source LLC
Chambersburg PA
CBHW061133160726
48006CB00037B/1988